My name: _____

My address: _____

My birth date: _____

*Here you can put
a photo of yourself.*

My club: _____

My team: _____

My coach: _____

Successes: _____

TRAINING FIELD HOCKEY

Katrin Barth/Lutz Nordmann

Sports Science Consultant: Dr. Berndt Barth

Meyer & Meyer Sport

Original Title: *Ich trainiere Hockey*
© Aachen: Meyer & Meyer, 2006
Translated by Petra Haynes
AAA Translation, St. Louis, Missouri, USA
www.AAATranslation.com

British Library Cataloguing in Publication Data
A catalogue record for this book is available from the British Library

Training Field Hockey
Katrin Barth /Lutz Nordmann
Oxford: Meyer & Meyer Sport (UK) Ltd., 2007
ISBN: 978-1-84126-223-9

© 2007 by Meyer & Meyer Sport (UK) Ltd.
Aachen, Adelaide, Auckland, Budapest, Graz, Indianapolis, Johannesburg,
New York, Olten (CH), Oxford, Singapore, Toronto
 Member of the World
Sport Publishers' Association (WSPA)
www.w-s-p-a.org
Printed and bound by: B.O.S.S Druck und Medien GmbH, Germany
ISBN: 978-1-84126-223-9
E-Mail: verlag@m-m-sports.com
www.m-m-sports.com

TABLE OF CONTENTS

Please note:
The exercises and practical suggestions in this book have been carefully chosen and reviewed by the authors. However, the authors are not liable for accidents or damages of any kind incurred in connection with the content of this book.

HI, IT'S ME, ELO THE ELEPHANT!
I HAVE THE WORLD'S BEST HOCKEY STICK
BECAUSE IT IS ATTACHED TO ME!

MAYBE YOU ALREADY KNOW ME FROM THE BOOK
"LEARNING FIELD HOCKEY."

NOW, DO YOU WANT TO GET SERIOUS
ABOUT TRAINING?
OK, I'M WITH YOU!

SOME SYMBOLS YOU WILL SEE A LOT IN THIS BOOK

Whenever you see the thumb, it means we have a tip for you.

You will get advice or a mistake will be pointed out to you.

At this place, you will find brainteasers or questions. The answers and solutions are at the back of the book.

Successful field hockey players must also practice outside of regularly scheduled practice sessions. In this book, you will find exercises that can also be done alone and at home.

Here you will find something to fill in, record or complete.

(Of course, you should only write in the book if it is your personal copy.)

. . . . *1 DEAR FIELD HOCKEY PLAYER*

Many girls and boys are ball-crazy from the time they are young children. As soon as they see a ball they have to pick it up, throw it, kick it or push it along with sticks. And if there is anything resembling a goal in the area, then goal fever sets in! That's probably how you, too, became interested in ball sports, and particularly in field hockey. Maybe you even practiced with our beginning book *Learning Field Hockey*.

In the beginning, field hockey can be played at home in the backyard, in the schoolyard, at the park, or wherever. Most of the time, a suitable patch of grass or playing surface with goals can be found.

Later, when you have decided to learn more, to train for field hockey and maybe even become a successful field hockey player, it will be time to join a hockey club. There you will train under the direction of trainers and coaches who are well trained, who may have been good players themselves, and who know how to teach children and adolescents how to handle a hockey stick. At a club, you can play and practice better with friends and teammates and learn a lot from others.

And, of course, the best part is that after all that training you get to start in a tournament with a well-prepared team. You will be an awesome team and everyone will do their best; together you will celebrate your victories and bolster each other's spirits when you lose.

But first a little story:

A healthy boy was visiting the mountains and wanted to climb a high peak. Cheerfully, he packed food and drink, and started to hike with a bounce in his step.

Since he wasn't familiar with the route, he made slow progress. He climbed up and when he realized that he couldn't get any further, he had to turn back and start over. These detours cost him lots of strength. Sometimes he got lucky and found a trail that brought him a little closer to the top. After many such attempts, he finally reached the summit, only to realize that others were already there. They told him about a good hiking trail. He could have taken that without all those detours.

Why didn't he use a map or ask someone who had already taken this hike?

Field hockey training is similar to our story about the "conqueror of the peaks." Many field hockey players have trained before you, and some have become very successful. You don't have to reinvent field hockey and field hockey training, but instead should learn from the experiences of players before you. It will make it much easier for you.

The training book *Training Field Hockey* will provide you with a kind of "trail map" and a little tutorial on how you can climb the "field hockey peak" without making a lot of detours. And of course there's your trainer who can show you the right way.

It sometimes happens that experienced field hockey players, trainers and book writers have slightly different opinions with regard to correct training. That is normal. Ask questions if you are not clear on something and find out the reasons behind different opinions. If we are mistaken about something or the development has simply progressed, make notes directly in your book.

Before you go to bed at night with the book under your pillow, thinking that's how you will win tomorrow, we just want to tell you:

We want to help you and explain how you can train properly. But you must train on your own. Whether or not you reach your goal and make it to the peak is mainly up to you.

There are different rules for playing field hockey indoors, on a small field or on a regular field, that you as a player must be familiar with. The techniques we will be talking about almost always apply to all types of play. Occasionally, we will point out restrictions.

Anything in this book pertaining to training applies to girls as well as boys. But to keep it simple we will refer to field hockey players or athletes in general. That means that the trainer, of course, also refers to female trainers.

We hope you have lots of fun with this book. It will certainly provide you with lots of interesting information to accompany you on a hopefully quick and safe trip to "the field hockey summit." We wish you lots of success!

Elo and the authors

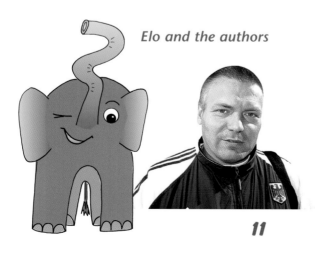

SPORTS AND ART

Sports and athletes are popular themes with many artists. The creation of many paintings, drawings, caricatures, sculptures and photographs was and is inspired by the elegance of movement, the physical beauty, speed, strength, and the fun of it.

Have you ever seen such a piece of sports art? Pay attention the next time you look through a magazine or visit a public building or a museum.

(You haven't hit me yet today! – What's wrong with you?)

(The world is a ball, and field hockey is its game)

On this page, you can see two field hockey drawings by the well-known German artist Peter-T. Schulz (Mülheim an der Ruhr, Germany).

.........2 FIELD HOCKEY – THEN AND NOW

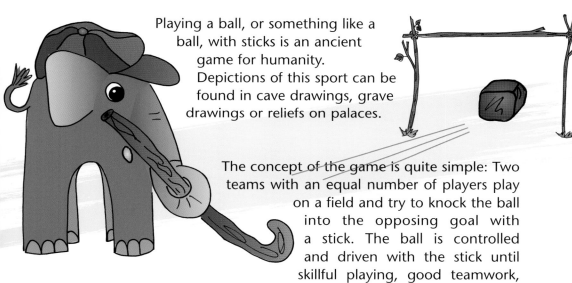

Playing a ball, or something like a ball, with sticks is an ancient game for humanity. Depictions of this sport can be found in cave drawings, grave drawings or reliefs on palaces.

The concept of the game is quite simple: Two teams with an equal number of players play on a field and try to knock the ball into the opposing goal with a stick. The ball is controlled and driven with the stick until skillful playing, good teamwork, outsmarting the opposing players and a great shooting technique causes it to land in the opposing goal. Whoever can do this best is the winner of the game.

Of course everyone can play as he likes and deems the most fun, but all of the players must be in agreement. But private agreements won't be sufficient when playing official or international tournaments. Standardized regulations are necessary. These apply to the size of the playing field, goals, times, number of players, substitutions, game rules, etc.

You can look all of this up in the body of rules and regulations of the USFHA and the international organization FIH. Of course these rules must always be updated and adapted.

DID YOU KNOW ...

...THAT STICKBALL GAMES HAVE ALWAYS BEEN A VERY POPULAR GAME DURING ALL ERAS AND IN ALL PARTS OF THE WORLD?

... THAT HOCKEY IS THE OLDEST OF THE OLYMPIC SPORTS STILL PLAYED TODAY?

... THAT THE PRECURSORS OF TODAY'S HOCKEY GAME WERE ALREADY MENTIONED IN ANCIENT PERSIAN HEROIC MYTHS (APPROX. 500 YEARS B.C.E.?) BACK THEN IT WAS A GAME OF THE RULING CLASS.

... THAT THROUGHOUT HISTORY THE PRECURSORS OF TODAY'S HOCKEY GAME APPEAR UNDER A VARIETY OF DIFFERENT NAMES? FOR EXAMPLE, THERE ARE BANDY, CAMAN, CHENDU, DAKIU, GICCHO, HOQUET, HURLING, KATHI, KOKI, LACROSSE, MAIL, POLO, AND SHINNEY.

... THAT IN 1832 FIELD HOCKEY BECAME MANDATORY IN ENGLISH GIRLS SCHOOLS?

... THAT DURING THE MIDDLE AGES, STICK GAMES WERE OFTEN ROUGH AND WILD FIGHTS? IN GREAT BRITAIN, DURING THE 19TH CENTURY, THESE GAMES WERE GRADUALLY TRANSFORMED INTO MODERN HOCKEY AND REFINED. THE FIRST BODY OF RULES AND REGULATIONS WAS PUBLISHED IN 1852.

... THAT THE FIRST HOCKEY CLUB WAS FOUNDED IN GREAT BRITAIN IN 1861? IT WAS CALLED "BLACKHEATH." THE "BALL" THEY PLAYED WITH WAS ACTUALLY A HARD RUBBER CUBE.

... THAT THE MODERN GAME OF HOCKEY FIRST CAME TO THE UNITED STATES IN 1901? THE BRITISH P.E. TEACHER M. K. APPLEBEE INTRODUCED IT AT HARVARD UNIVERSITY.

... THAT THE RULES WERE CONTINUOUSLY CHANGED AND ADAPTED OVER THE COURSE OF THE 19TH CENTURY? FINALLY THERE WAS AN ACTUAL ROUND BALL INSTEAD OF THE CUBE. THE HANDS COULD NO LONGER BE USED FOR PLAYING AND THE STICK HAD TO STAY BELOW SHOULDER LEVEL. ALSO, STANDARD TEAM SIZE WAS SET AT 11 PLAYERS AND THE SHOT CIRCLE WAS INTRODUCED.

...THAT HOCKEY WAS A DEMONSTRATION SPORT AT THE 1908 OLYMPICS IN LONDON? HOCKEY HAS BEEN AN OLYMPIC SPORT SINCE THE PARIS OLYMPICS IN 1924, AND WOMEN'S HOCKEY HAS BEEN PART OF IT SINCE THE MOSCOW OLYMPICS IN 1980.

... THAT IN THE EARLY YEARS, INDIA WON GOLD MEDALS SIX CONSECUTIVE TIMES? ONLY IN 1960 WAS PAKISTAN ABLE TO END THAT RUN.

... THAT UNTIL THE END OF THE 1950S, THE STICKS WERE MADE TO BE VERY ELASTIC? ELASTICITY WAS PARTICULARLY IMPORTANT ON A REAL GRASS SURFACE. IN ADDITION, THREE LAYERS OF RUBBER WERE ADDED TO THE WOOD FROM HICKORY OR MULBERRY TREES.

... THAT THE INTRODUCTION OF ARTIFICIAL TURF IN 1970 BROUGHT MANY CHANGES TO THE SPORT OF FIELD HOCKEY? FOR EXAMPLE, HOW HARD A HIT IS NO LONGER MATTERS AS MUCH, AND THE BALL IS DRIBBLED MORE.

... THAT "OFFSIDE" IN FIELD HOCKEY WAS ELIMINATED AFTER THE ATLANTA OLYMPICS IN 1996? THIS MADE THE GAME MORE ATTRACTIVE TO SPECTATORS AND SIMPLER FOR THE REFEREES.

... THAT THE CHANGES IN PLAYING TECHNIQUE ALSO PLACED HIGHER DEMANDS ON THE STICKS? THE FIH APPROVED FULLY SYNTHETIC STICKS IN 1999.

CURRENT LIST OF THE WORLD'S TOP TEAMS

It is fun to track which teams are the best. Here is a listing of the most important international tournaments, and you can write the current best teams in the blank spaces. Write the names and dates with pencil so you can keep updating your list.

Competition	Year	Women	Men
Olympic Championships			
European Championships Field			
European Championships Indoor			
World Championships Field			
World Championships Indoor			
Champions Trophy			
European Masters Field			
European Cup-Winners Cup Field			
European Cup Indoor			

THIS IS HOW FIELD HOCKEY IS ORGANIZED

Every country has a national organization for its field hockey players.

Do you know the name of your national association?

Write it down here.

Put the logo here.

THIS IS HOW FIELD HOCKEY IS ORGANIZED ON THE INTERNATIONAL LEVEL

The worldwide organization for all field hockey players is the **Fédération International de Hockey** (**FIH** for short).

The FIH was founded on January 7, 1924, in Paris. It currently counts 106 national organizations as members.

The European field hockey organization is the **European Hockey Federation** (**EHF** for short).

If you want to know more, look on the Internet!

www.fihockey.org
www.eurohockey.org
www.usfieldhockey.com
www.hockey-coach.de

17

FAN PAGE

Which successful player would you like to interview?

_____

What would you ask him?

_____

_____

_____

Here is a place for you to paste photos of your idols or collect autographs.

. . . . .3 HI THERE, TINA BACHMANN!

Born August 1, 1978, in Mülheim a. d. Ruhr, Germany
Student of elementary education
Trainer certificate from the Trainerakademie of the German Olympic Sports
  Federation in Cologne, Germany
Player on the German national team, Olympic champion 2004 in Athens

Tina, you are a super-successful field hockey player! What's your secret?
When you have a goal, it means buckling down and hanging in there, even when sometimes the goal seems to be far away!

How did you manage to stick with the training for so long?
When you know why you are doing it, why you are training so hard, and you have a big goal, then you can handle a lot. Besides, I have experienced some of those great moments when dreams come true. That's when you know that all the training is worth it!

Why did you choose to play field hockey in particular?
Because to me field hockey is the best, fastest and most elegant ball sport. Besides, I am carrying on a family tradition. My father, Gerd Bachmann, played 108 international games for Germany. That's what I want to do, too!

Has field hockey training helped you in other areas of your life?
A sport is like "school" for the rest of your life! To be successful in a sport, you need discipline, endurance, will power and perseverance. Add to that diligence, organization and reliability. Especially in a team sport, you have to adjust to your teammates, to assert yourself and lead, but also to adapt and subordinate yourself.

With all that training, do you still have time for leisure time and hobbies?
Of course you have to train a lot when you have big athletic goals. After sport and studies, there isn't much time left over for other things. Nevertheless, it is important to have balance and take an occasional time out to do something totally different. I like to get together with friends, visit my family, go to the movies or shopping.

What is your advice to young field hockey players?
Always stick with it and train hard! When you give it your all, sooner or later it will pay off!

Thank you very much for the interview and lots of luck in the future!

Greetings and lots of success

. . . . .4 TRAINING – THE ROAD TO SUCCESS

To play like the top players would be the best! You want to be able to guide the hockey ball accurately and confidently, to stop it with ease, to hit it hard and with precision. You want to score amazing goals and be confident in defense.

Surely you have noticed during practice and at games that things don't always go as well as you wish. When receiving a ball you don't always get it under control right away, a pass is sometimes a little off, and your shots at goal lack some bite. You could also have more strength left for running during the second half, and your fear of hard opposing balls hasn't quite gone away, either.

You have noticed that others can also play pretty well, some better than you. But that is not a problem because what others can do, you can do, too. But what can you do to become a good and maybe even a top player, or a successful player at the national level? The truth is, you have to train hard if you want to improve in field hockey. With this training book, we would like to help you train successfully.

Don't worry! No one was ever born a champion! The others had to start out the same way, and they have only gotten this far with lots of training.

THE WAY TO THE TOP

This book won't be able to replace your trainer. But it will explain why your trainer works on field hockey technique and body conditioning with you, and why he says that you need to improve your endurance, your speed and your flexibility.

You will learn to understand why it is necessary to also do other exercises that don't appear to have anything to do with field hockey, in addition to playing field hockey on goals.

You will recognize how important it is to warm up and stretch before training or a game. And you find out why you have to cool down and stretch after practicing.

In addition, you will get suggestions as to what you can do yourself, in training and outside of the regular training sessions, to improve your performance and independently monitor and evaluate your progress. The top field hockey players can do that very well. After many years of training and many hockey games, they know exactly whether or not they are in shape, what their strengths and weaknesses are, and what they have to work on to play even better.

To the athlete, the trainer then becomes a good friend and counselor who sometimes also has to be strict when the "weaker inner self" says, "That's just too hard today. I quit!"

TRAINING ACTIVELY, CONSCIOUSLY AND JOYFULLY

Field hockey training is anything one does **actively** and **consciously** to be able to play better. But what does that mean?

- **Actively** means that you **yourself** have to train. You don't get better by having your trainer do ball control and hitting exercises. You also do not improve by putting the field hockey book under your pillow at night, but only by actually training **yourself**, meaning, by being active.

- **Consciously** means that you understand the purpose and benefit of the tasks the trainer gives you and carry them out independently. That you may already think up training tasks of your own and carry them out.

You should not only be doing what you are told, but you should also know why you are doing it, which is good for your success. When you know why you are doing something, you enjoy it more and stick with it longer.

Since a field hockey player has to train many years to achieve good performances, it makes sense to find out at the beginning what it means to train properly and to learn how to train. You will make more progress and training will be much more fun.

TRAINING RIGHT – BUT HOW?

A prerequisite for conscious training is answering these three questions:

- **What do I want to achieve?**

- **Why do I want to train?**

- **How should I train?**

What do I want to achieve? What are my training goals?

Active and conscious training requires specific goals. If you don't have a goal, training soon won't be fun anymore. A field hockey player's most important goal is of course to enjoy playing field hockey. But in the long term, it will only be fun if you get a better feel for the ball, the tempo and the game situation. With a versatile field hockey technique, you will master the most difficult situations, reach every ball and make dangerous shots at goal. This will make you a reliable member of the team who helps the team win. Or would you like to always be the worst one and always blame yourself for losing?

Maybe you set a really big goal right away. The games at the Olympics are shown on television or you are watching the big tournaments. The players are intensely focused and technically perfect. The passes to the teammates are accurate and hard; they cleanly take the ball away from their opponent and end up with a super flick.
Everyone cheers, marvels and is thrilled. Now you think: "I want to do that, too."

And that's the way it should be! But you do have to bear in mind that dreaming of success doesn't make it real. It will take lots of sweat first, and next to some small successes you will suffer many defeats along the way.

Next to the big goals that are still off in the distant future, you also set some short-term goals. For example, you may resolve to make your shots at goal more accurate, to be more solid on defense, or to cheat less during fitness training. It is fun to reach the goals you have set, and if it isn't working just yet, it is an incentive. However, don't set impossible goals for yourself, but only those that are realistic and that you can achieve in the near future.

Goals are the impetus of every successful athlete! In field hockey, we differentiate between team goals (we want to move up, we want to be more attentive in team play...) and the goals every player sets for himself.

The following pages focus primarily on these individual goals.

DOESN'T THE TRAINER HAVE TO SET THE GOALS?

Maybe you think that it is the trainer's job. He can tell you what you can and should achieve. He will do that. He sets training goals for his athletes and he designs training plans and trains with them according to these plans.

But every field hockey player knows himself best, knows his strengths and weaknesses. That is why he also knows best which goals to set for himself. It is always better to set your own goals, rather than have them "pressed upon you" by someone else. Then they are your own goals and you are much more willing to do everything to achieve them. If you can tell your trainer exactly what isn't working so well yet and what you want to really work on in the near future, then he can respond by helping you train.

Imagine yourself in the following situations while training with a new trainer. How would you react?

1 Your trainer tells you to dribble the ball from the quarter line into the shot circle at a full run and then hit it hard into the long corner of the goal. This is too difficult for you because you have only just learned how to hit. Yesterday, you couldn't even hit the ball between two markers.

2 The field season starts up again after summer vacation and technique training is part of the program. The trainer asks you to flick a non-moving ball over a distance of 35 feet. But you spent the last two weeks of vacation at a training camp, and there you already flicked from the centerline all the way to the opposing quarter line.

Write your goals along with the date in the chart on page 27. In the second column, add the date you want to achieve the goal by.

Once you have actually achieved it, you can check it off and write down the real date.

Of course trainers and athletes sometimes have different opinions. In part, there is some inconsistency between the goals you set for yourself and those the trainer sets for you. It isn't easy for the trainer. If, in your opinion, his expectations are too high, it means he has a lot of confidence in you but is asking too much of you. If you think his expectations for you are too low, show him that you are capable of more.

What I want to achieve / Date	Target Date / Made it!
Paired passes (push / low hit) without losing the ball, number over ...	(01.08) 01.16
To make 2000 m in the Cooper test (12 min.)	

When the list is full, draw a new chart and lay or paste it in the book. But you can also start a "goal notebook" that you can use over a longer period of time.

THE OVERALL GOAL AND THE SUB-GOALS

At the last game, Tom made a lot of mistakes as the game progressed. In doing so, he did not meet the expectations of the trainer, his team, the club, his parents, and not his own. But he also knows the reason, namely his lack of strength and endurance.

He has resolved to increase his strength in the near future. That is his overall goal. But of course he won't be able to immediately strengthen all areas of his body simultaneously during the first few training sessions. That is why he has set sub-goals that will take him to his overall goal.

Here you can see what that means:

STRENGTHENING THE TRUNK MUSCLES (ABDOMINALS AND BACK)

OVERALL STRENGTHENING OF THE LEG MUSCLES

OVERALL STRENGTHENING OF THE SHOULDER AND ARM MUSCLES

INCREASING POWER

INCREASING SUCCESS OF ATTACKS

VARYING STRENGTH EXERTION AND SITUATION-APPROPRIATE ACTIONS

LOW-STRENGTH ENDURANCE   *HIGH-STRENGTH ENDURANCE*

This is how you can set sub-goals for all fitness-related abilities, attack and defense techniques, competitive strength, etc. Think about which sub-goals will take you to your overall goal. You can talk about this with your trainer.

It is good for your motivation to have occasional successes – even if they are only sub-goals!

Why do I want to train in field hockey? What are the motives?

The reason or the motives for the training is the "psychological motor" that initiates the training. They determine whether or not you go to practice, and whether you fight or just give up when you fail.

Going to practice is never a problem when the weather is bad and you are bored. You want to meet up with your teammates and your trainer may have something exciting planned. But what happens when the sun is shining, your friends are going out for ice cream, or there is great show on television? Is your gym bag packed as quickly then?

But if you really want to reach a sub-goal and you know that the next training session is particularly important for the team line up, or the upcoming tournament is particularly important, then the decision won't be that hard to make.

I GO TO PRACTICE AND TRY TO DO MY BEST

	Very important reason	Important reason	Not that important
Because I love team play.	☐	☐	☐
Because I want to do something for my health.	☐	☐	☐
Because I want to play on a successful team.	☐	☐	☐
Because my parents want me to.	☐	☐	☐
Because my friend is going, too.	☐	☐	☐
Because I don't want to disappoint my trainer.	☐	☐	☐
Because I enjoy being in a great training group.	☐	☐	☐
Because I don't have anything else to do.	☐	☐	☐
Because you need a lot of "brains" for field hockey.	☐	☐	☐
Because I'm fast and nimble.	☐	☐	☐
Because I want to be in the paper.	☐	☐	☐
Because I want to make the national team.	☐	☐	☐
Because I am building character through training.	☐	☐	☐
Because field hockey is just awesome.	☐	☐	☐
Because _____	☐	☐	☐
Because _____	☐	☐	☐

Ask yourself why you go to practice and work so hard. Decide how important a motive is to you. Check the appropriate column on the list on page 30. If you have any other reasons, list them on the two blank lines.

The trainer tells Max: "Run the 60 yards as fast as you can!" Max gets a good start and runs as fast as he can, giving it his all. After the run, he is pretty satisfied with his performance.

Tina runs next. The trainer clocks her with a faster time. This annoys Max who had been pretty satisfied with his result. Now Max wants to compete against Tina directly because he doesn't like to be beaten (especially by a girl).

In the end, the final result doesn't really matter because, as you can imagine, Max ran even faster and more focused than he did before. The direct competition with Tina motivated him to become even faster.

A very important reason for exertion in training is that you know why you have to carry out the various exercises and how you can improve your performance by doing so.

Anything you do with interest goes twice, as well!

How do I train to achieve my goals?

The exertion in training that is supposed to improve performance is called load. Just like every field hockey player is different, so is his capacity and the capacity required to improve his performance. If an athlete does not exert himself sufficiently in training, his performance will not improve, and if he exerts himself too much, exhaustion and loss of concentration can cause injuries. Unfortunately, there is no chart for

the player or the trainer to look up how high the load must and can be. Every athlete has to help with that. Over time, he learns to "listen" to his body and recognize when the load is sufficiently high. The correct training load will lead to a performance increase because the body adapts. Thus the heart increases its size and capacity, the muscles get stronger and you are able to fully concentrate over a longer period of time. After a period of regular training, you also notice that exercises that previously got you really winded are no longer as strenuous. If you used to be really exhausted after halftime, you may now be able to hang in there longer.

Many sport scientists and doctors have done research on which training methods would be most beneficial to field hockey players in order to achieve a maximum athletic performance and keep the body healthy and fit. Just training randomly does not produce the desired results. It can even do damage.

Surely you have noticed that your performance drops when you don't practice for a while. At the first practice session after a break, the motion sequences and exercises seemed much more difficult and your performance wasn't as good. So you had to start back with a lesser load than what you had ended the last practice session with.

Regular training is better than irregular training!

Do you remember our example of the hockey summit you want to reach? Laziness and irregularity in training interrupt performance development. You are thrown back a ways on your road to success. It's as if you slid back down a part of the road you had already covered.

But often it isn't possible to train as diligently as you intended to. There are times when you have to study more for school or you are on vacation with your parents. Or maybe there aren't enough open time slots for the field or gym.

But anyone with an athletic goal should practice regularly. Of course that includes endurance training, flexibility, strength exercises and calisthenics. If you cannot train due to illness or injury, you must rest until you are well again. But if you cannot train because you are on vacation, or due to a school event, or for other reasons, try to still stay in shape.

Go jogging, do strength exercises, do exercises to improve your feel for the ball or stretch indoors, or work on your flexibility. Use the summer to train your endurance and strength with swimming, paddling, inline skating or mountain biking, and go skiing in winter. That will make catching up after a break easier.

WHAT IT TAKES TO BE A GOOD FIELD HOCKEY PLAYER

Perhaps you can think of many good answers to this question. There are many things a good field hockey player must be able to do, have and know. In this chart, we attempt to illustrate everything that impacts the performance of a player and what has to be trained.

The individual factors definitely cannot be viewed independent of each other. That is why, in the illustration, the circles also overlap. The circle for mental abilities surrounds everything because they affect everything. In addition, there are important exterior influences, which you can see on the outer arrows.

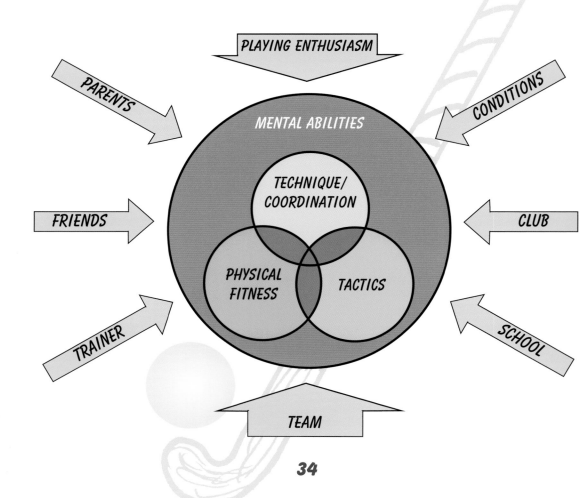

Technique and good coordination refer to the movements that are typical in field hockey. These include the various options for receiving and controlling the ball, shooting at goal, as well as the necessary body control.

A field hockey player who has good endurance, strength, and speed flexibillity, is said to have a high level of **physical fitness**. In a game, you want to quickly reach the ball, nimbly dribble around the opponent, and score a goal with a powerful hit. For that, you have to be totally fit and focused throughout the entire game or tournament.

Tactic is the plan that can help you defeat your opponent. Which technique would be more successful in which situation? How can you play to your strengths, and how do you arrange play within the team?

How confident, strong or timid you are, whether you are discouraged by a goal by the opposition or a bad pass, or if you are spurred on to really fight, depends on your **psyche**. Nervousness should be converted to particular attentiveness and playing enjoyment.

Our chart also shows arrows like **parents, friends, trainer, conditions, club and school**. (One could easily add more.) Those are the influences that come from the outside and affect the player's performance. It matters greatly whether the parents support your training or are against it. How you get along with the trainer and your teammates is also significant. Problems at school, disagreements with friends or family stress do not allow you to have a clear head. It is great when many spectators are cheering, the field is in good condition and the sun is shining. And without the necessary playing enthusiasm, you likely won't achieve top performances.

All factors combine to bring success

Field hockey is demanding in terms of endurance, speed, and arm and leg strength. That is why physical fitness is so important. But physical fitness alone does not make you a successful player. And if all you have is perfect technique or amazing tactics, you won't be able to help your team. A field hockey player must possess all of the factors. And when our control system – the psyche – fails us, everything can go topsy-turvy.

What does that mean in regard to your training?

The best training is to play, play, play! When playing a game, you can run, pass, dribble and make shots at goal. You have to demonstrate nerves of steel and determine which tactic is the most successful. Someone who plays a lot has the best chance to make advances in his performance. But if you notice a weakness in a particular area, some additional training will be necessary. In the following chapters, we will address the individual factors in more detail and discuss training methods. We will show you some options for exercises you can do at home for self-monitoring and evaluation of your own performance. Discuss everything with your trainer, as well. He knows the ropes.

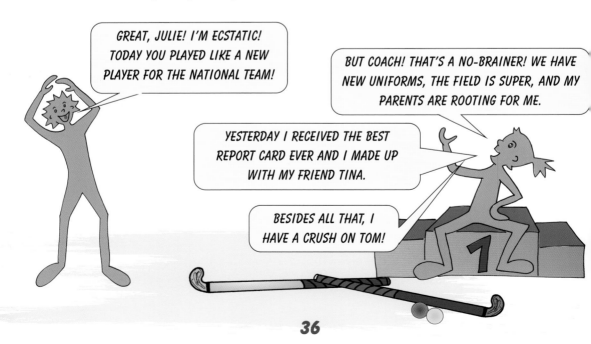

GREAT, JULIE! I'M ECSTATIC! TODAY YOU PLAYED LIKE A NEW PLAYER FOR THE NATIONAL TEAM!

BUT COACH! THAT'S A NO-BRAINER! WE HAVE NEW UNIFORMS, THE FIELD IS SUPER, AND MY PARENTS ARE ROOTING FOR ME.

YESTERDAY I RECEIVED THE BEST REPORT CARD EVER AND I MADE UP WITH MY FRIEND TINA.

BESIDES ALL THAT, I HAVE A CRUSH ON TOM!

. . . . .5 TECHNIQUE AND COORDINATION

To pass, receive and shoot, the player must constantly run to the correct position, nimbly dribble around the opponent and hit the ball hard. But all of the physical fitness that is absolutely necessary is useless if the motion is executed incorrectly. Only the right technique gives you the ability to control the ball.

Have you ever attempted to juggle five balls or bowling pins? Some acrobats use burning torches or sharp knives, which they balance while riding a bicycle. Even the best acrobats weren't able to do that in the cradle. Such skills require long and intensive training until one has mastered them perfectly. Just like that, a good field hockey player must master the playing techniques. Most often it is interplay between many individual little movements, that make up a certain technique.

New techniques are always added in further training, and you will increasingly refine familiar techniques.

During a game, the movements must happen automatically!

You need all of your strength during a strenuous game; you need to concentrate on your tasks, and follow the action because the tension increases with a close score in the second half. You don't have time to think about which leg comes forward, which hand grips the stick at the top and at the bottom, or how to swing the stick. All of that has to happen automatically.

The technique has to be practiced until it works perfectly. During training, you will practice the techniques and the motion sequences over and over in many different ways, until you no longer have to think about every single step. Imagine if you had to think about the motion sequence before every action.

Straddle position, left foot forward, stick position 45°, weight on the left leg, bring stick to the knee... etc.

TECHNIQUE TRAINING

When you learn a new technique, it is usually introduced via an explanation and a demonstration by the trainer. He explains the motion sequence, tells you what you have to pay particular attention to and what mistakes to avoid.

Just like in school, there are different methods for learning. As people are different, they also have different ways of learning or memorizing something new. The trainer will work with the different learning types and introduce new material through a variety of methods. Often it is a combination of different ways of learning that is successful.

Examples of different methods:

- The trainer explains the new technique.
- The trainer or another player demonstrates the technique.
- The new technique is shown via drawings or sequence pictures.
- Possible mistakes are discussed with the aid of error images.
- Videos are shown.
- The trainer asks the athletes to describe and explain the new technique.
- The athletes make sketches.
- They try the new technique themselves.
- The technique is executed with monitoring and suggestions by the trainer.
- The technique is executed with monitoring and suggestions by training buddies.
- The athletes do dry exercises without a ball.

What learning type are you? Check the learning methods that are most helpful to you when learning a new technique. Try out what works best for you!

PERSEVERANCE BRINGS SUCCESS

After the trainer's explanation and demonstration, it is your turn to practice the new material. Of course it is lots of fun to learn and execute a new technique. In the beginning, the movements tend to be fairly vague, and you are just trying to make sure that your arms and legs are doing it right. You quickly see some progress. Your movements become surer and faster.

But gradually all that practicing gets dull. You don't notice any obvious improvement in your performance anymore and the thrill of something new is gone as well. You think that things are already going pretty well with this new technique. Why keep practicing? Now comes the point when you may not feel like doing it anymore. But if you quit now, you will forget some things and all that previous practicing will have been for nothing. So remember what you have resolved to do and fight your "inner couch potato!"

The road to increased performance

After that quick progress, there will be many training days when you will feel like nothing is happening. It is important to know that this stage will come. On the long road to perfect technique, there are always stages of

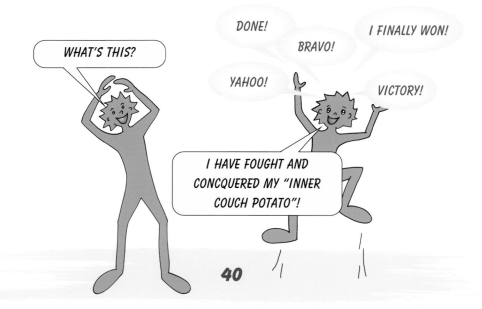

40

quick progress, and also stages of grinding drudgery. So if you think it can't get any better, that you have already reached your performance capacity and any more practice is useless, keep on trying and you will see that it does get better.

During this apparent standstill, your body is preparing for the next level of performance development. You could say it is getting internally reprogrammed for the next step. So don't let an apparent standstill drive you to despair. These are necessary transitional phases. The key is: Perseverance!

You will learn some techniques relatively quickly. Others require many, many hours of training, even years. Rest assured – persistent and arduous training pays off!

Tips for technique training

- Listen and watch closely when the technique is being explained, shown through pictures, and demonstrated.
- Mentally retrace the technique and, with your eyes closed, concentrate on visualizing the sequence and the movement.
- Practice the technique over and over again in training. Monitor yourself after every repetition.
- Ask to find out what you need to work on.
- Take your time looking over the illustrations and descriptions one more time and compare them to your own movements.
- Try to explain and show the technique to someone else.
- Monitor and help each other!

How a player practices to perfect a new technique is different for everyone. However, everyone has to practice a lot. In the end, the technique should be executed quickly, accurately and without progress monitoring, meaning automatically. The progressions are "programmed" and stored in your brain. It is almost like downloading a computer program that will later be accessed again.

If you don't work hard in training, and play unfocused and sloppy, the wrong sequences will be stored. When something incorrect has been automated, it will take a lot of effort to break that habit later.

MONITORING – EVALUATING – IMPROVING

Don't learn anything incorrect and automate it! To avoid this, you need to monitor the progression of a new technique, recognize the mistakes and execute the movement increasingly faster and more accurately. How quickly that works also depends on your goals and your motivation. Do you remember?

The trainer practiced flicks with the training group and now everyone can practice independently on the field. Jenny tries very hard. The trainer watches her and says, "Great, Jenny! You are doing well!" Jenny is happy and keeps practicing.

Several training sessions later, the trainer is again watching and says, "That doesn't look so great yet, Jenny. You're too stiff, and you are not hitting the ball correctly!" Now Jenny is upset. She did it exactly like last week. Then the trainer complimented her and now he is nagging!

As you have probably already guessed, the trainer in this story did not make a mistake. He only adapted his evaluation to the situation and the potentialities. Jenny's flicks certainly weren't perfect in the beginning. But they were pretty good for the first time. But later, after many repetitions, an improvement could be expected. The next sub-goal should be reached.

You reach many sub-goals on the road to perfect technique, and every little mistake should be observed and corrected. Evaluation by the trainer is best since he knows the most about playing field hockey.

MUSCLE SENSE

Parents and teachers often talk about the five senses you should use when you want to learn something new. What they are trying to say is that you should listen well, watch carefully, touch the surface, smell it and taste it. Surely you have noticed that not all senses are always used simultaneously or equally.

Senses that are important in field hockey

You certainly can't taste anything when you play field hockey. Smelling is more of a secondary effect, like when spring is coming or when you walk into the locker room. That you need to see to play doesn't require an explanation. But during a competition, you also have to be able to hear: the contact with the ball, the rhythm of movement, the calls from teammates and the cheering of the spectators. Part of the sense organ called the ear includes your sense of balance. You need that to keep your balance during all of the movements.

Some people even talk about a sixth sense. Field hockey players need such a sixth sense for the muscle sense or sense of movement. We will simply call it **"muscle sense."** It is very important for learning and mastering technique in field hockey. During a game, you watch the ball, your teammates, and follow the opponent's actions. You can't look at how your feet are positioned or at what angle you are holding your stick. You must be able to "feel" these things. And this "feeling," or "muscle sense," is developed in training through regular practice.

COORDINATIVE ABILITIES

What actually happens during a single play? You watch the ball, follow the opponent's movements, look where your teammates are standing, decide how you will react in your position and with whom you could team up, run to the ball, sprint, take a swing … and then there is not a hit but a flick! Now quickly reorganize and react correctly!

In sports, we differentiate between various coordinative abilities.

Linking ability

As the word suggests, movements are linked, meaning they are connected to each other. This applies to the backswing, the swing and the hit on goal, or assuming a low body position, setting the stick down in backhand position and roofing it for a backhand stop. Add to that the linking of techniques within a certain play situation, such as receiving the ball, controlling the ball and shooting at goal, or running along, receiving the ball and dribbling on.

Orientation ability

Your situation and the positions of your teammates on the field are constantly changing. The ball comes from all different directions. Will the ball be passed to you or will it go out of bounds? You constantly have to adjust your position, running speed and stick position accordingly. That allows you to react ideally in every situation.

Adaptability and adjustability

During a game the situation constantly changes. You constantly want to adjust to that. But unexpected things often happen: The ball comes in different than expected; your teammate reacts too late, and in addition you have to constantly switch from attack to defense, etc.

Balance

A wide straddle, a lunge, optimum range, nimble dribbling and that fast sprint to the ball – you are constantly changing your position and center of gravity. It is important to keep your balance while doing so. This allows you to react confidently and quickly in any situation.

Rhythmic ability

In field hockey, there are movements that always repeat themselves in a certain sequence: i.e., forehand-backhand ball control or backswing – accelerating – connecting – completing the swing. There is a noticeable rhythm there, which can help you in the execution.

Reaction ability

This is the ability to recognize a situation and react quickly with the right movement at the appropriate speed. You get yourself open and choose the appropriate mode for receiving the ball.

Differentiation ability

This is the player's ability to recognize whether he needs to hit the ball hard or soft, long or short. It is also the ability to choose the stick angle so the ball has the desired height. The player also recognizes whether the ball bounces and will need to be stopped with a high stick, or whether he should lay down a plank.

BALANCE EXERCISES

With your eyes closed
Stand up straight and close your eyes,
- *Hold your arms out to the side.*
- *Extend your arms overhead.*
- *Take a lunge step forward / to the side and back.*

Standing on one leg
- *Switch legs – first the right, then the left.*
- *Close your eyes at the same time.*
- *Extend your arms out to the side and then overhead.*

Standing on a shaky surface
- *Stand on a mat, a pillow or a rolled-up blanket.*
- *Stand on a narrow (fallen) log.*
- *Stand on a core board or a sports gyroscope.*

Now with power: One on one
- *Stand back to back with a partner. Who will win the "pushing duel"?*

- *You and a partner get in flick position. Who will win the "pushing duel"?*

........6 PHYSICAL FITNESS

Max visits the doctor because he thinks that something is not quite right with his body. "I don't know what's wrong with me. Yesterday we practiced passing. I was totally exhausted and at the end I was barely able to stay on my feet. My thighs hurt and my arms were cramping!"

"You most likely didn't train enough!"

"But I go to practice three times a week. There I practice the techniques for receiving, defense and shooting at goal."

"And what else do you do for training?"

"What do you mean? I'm playing the entire time!"

What will the doctor tell Max? Probably that his training is too one-sided. He forgot about fitness training. He has no endurance, no strength, and he isn't flexible. His body cannot handle the regular training with intense load-bearing phases.

WHAT PHYSICAL FITNESS MEANS

In sports, the term "physical fitness" refers primarily to physical abilities. Your fitness level determines how much endurance and speed you have, how strong you are and how much physical strain you can handle. You can tell whether your fitness level is good or not by, for instance, how quickly you get winded after a short sprint, how long you can bear up under athletic strain without all of your limbs hurting, with how much power you sprint or hit and how flexible you are.

You get physically fit through regular field hockey training. But you can also get fit and improve your fitness by engaging in many other supplementary sports.

FITNESS-RELATED ABILITIES

We will now take a closer look at the most important fitness-related abilities a field hockey player must have to be in all-around good shape. They include:

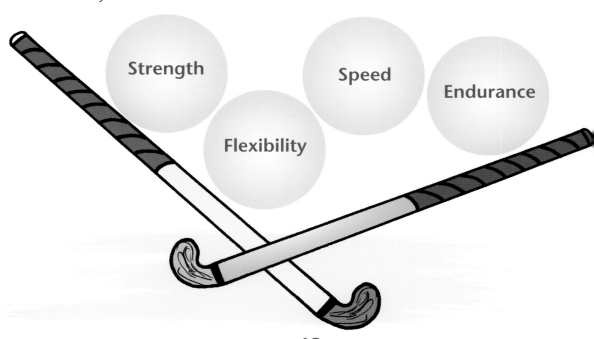

Strength

Speed

Endurance

Flexibility

Endurance

Endurance is the fitness-related ability one needs to handle long-term physical strain. That includes not getting tired quickly from strenuous training, a long game, a tournament day or even during trips to competitions. Your body should also be able to recover quickly after greater physical strain. That is called **regeneration**.

When you play field hockey you are constantly running back and forth. You guide the ball, try to intercept the opposing attacker or try to get open. Someone who wants to play successfully must maintain the fast tempo and concentrate until the final whistle.

Someone who has poor endurance, who cannot make it through a game and constantly takes breaks, hurts his team!

Of course the best endurance training is when you really utilize the practice sessions with your team and participate fully. But you should also work on your endurance off the hockey field. That includes jogging regularly, biking swimming, and skiing, or playing other ball games.

Speed

Speed is the ability you need to execute a movement with the most acceleration and speed possible. Critical here is the fastest possible muscle response (contraction of muscles).

A field hockey game "lives" from fast sprints, sudden turns and unexpected passes. If the situation is right, the player wants to react as quickly as lightning.

Someone who is too slow and always reacts too late, most often losing his one-on-one battles, is an unreliable partner and not a competitive player.

For example, a field hockey payer needs:

Reaction speed: As a player, you need the ability to instantly react to new, unexpected situations and surprising actions by the opponent.

Action speed: Once you have identified a situation you must decide how to act and react as quickly as possible.

Movement speed: You can quickly execute the movement or the required technique.

In training, you also have to execute all movements quickly. Someone who always moves in "slow motion" and at half strength will not be much faster in a game either!

Outside of your training on the hockey field, you can also work on your speed with a variety of sports like tennis, badminton, volleyball, soccer, etc.

In addition, you should always do intermittent sprints when you are jogging.

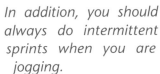

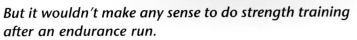

But it wouldn't make any sense to do strength training after an endurance run.

When doing speed training it is important that, in addition to a good warm-up, you are not wiped out and tired.

50

Strength

Strength is necessary for moving something heavy, like lifting, pushing, pulling or pressing weights. Without strength, it is not possible to execute movements, particularly athletic movements. You also need strength to hold your body or parts of your body in a certain position, to move them as fast as possible or to slow down a movement.

As a field hockey player, you need lots of leg strength for fast sprints and the low body position. Strong arms and hands are also important to handling the stick easily and hitting it hard. Strong back and stomach muscles are important to better handling the special stresses and strains.

A top player knows exactly how much strength he needs to play the ball in order to reach a certain distance and height. That is the result of lots of training and playing experience.

Perhaps you have seen the many apparatuses fitness studios have for athletes to steel their muscles on. But to get in good shape, you would be better off using a rubber resistance band, simple weights, and especially your own body weight.

There are many exercises you can also do at home: Push-ups, sit-ups, climbing up stairs, exercises with a rubber resistance band, high jumping, etc.

ENDURANCE EXERCISES

Here are some options for working on your endurance. Watch out for traffic!

Distance running
Choose a regular route of approximately. 1.5 miles. If you want to know the exact distance, you can measure it with an odometer from a bicycle or car. But it is sufficient to estimate the distance. Of course, it can be longer, too. Important for performance monitoring is that you always run the same route. Write down your times once a week.

Sprint exercises
When you are jogging, break from your steady pace into short sprints. Look for trees, street signs or intersections as start and finish markers. Run the distance in between as fast as you can.

Mark a stretch of 10 – 30 yards along a path or a quiet street (make sure that you can always find the markings again). Find a helper who can time your sprints and give the start signal.

Other sports
Many other sports require good endurance. Add a little variety to your training plan:

- Ski
- Bike
- Swim
- Play soccer
- Play tennis
- other

ATHLETIC TESTS

30 m sprints
A 30 m stretch is run twice. The start is signaled with a whistle. The average time – (1. time + 2. time) ÷ 2 – is recorded.

10 m sprints
The time for a 10 m sprint can be taken on the 30 m stretch.

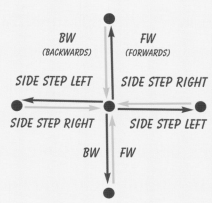

Star pattern run 5 x 5 m
You run the prepared "star" in the manner indicated. You look straight ahead and the marking has to be touched with each change in direction.

Shuttle sprint
The markings are set up as shown on the sketch. You start running with the stick and ball and set the ball down on the marking,
● then run back. When you pass the ball again,
● you pick it up and set it down at the next marking.

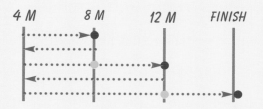

Individual runs are timed.

In races against a partner, the first person to finish wins.

Cooper test (run as many meters as possible in 12 minutes)
Run 12 minutes on a 400 m track. Try to run as many meters as possible during that time period.

Jumping left, right from a standing position
You stand at the starting line and jump without a running start, alternating left – right – left – right – landing on both feet. The distance is measured.

STRENGTHENING BACK AND STOMACH MUSCLES

The special movements in field hockey, like sprinting, stopping, turning, swinging and hitting hard, require strong muscles that can handle all of these things. Strong back and stomach muscles in particular help prevent physical damage.

"Horse back"

"Cat back"

You lie on your back and lift your pelvis off the floor. Chest, stomach, thighs and knees form a straight line.

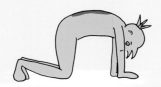

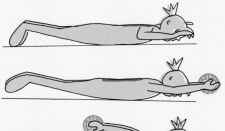

Lie flat on your stomach, bend your arms and lift your arms and head slightly off the floor. Keep your eyes on the floor.

Hold the ball with your arms extended. Lift your arms and legs slightly off the floor.

Hold the ball above your rear. Pass it from hand to hand.

Lie on your back and bend your knees. Your back is firmly on the floor. Now try to lift your torso slightly off the floor.

Now elevate your legs.

Exercises to strengthen the trunk muscles should be a regular part of your training program.

EXERCISES FOR STRONG HANDS AND WRISTS

The stick forms a roof, is slightly canted or swings. You learn the ideal technique in training. But the best technique is useless if you don't have the strength to hold the stick firmly in place or to move it.

Do something for strong hands and wrists!

Strong hands
There are special rubber rings you can squeeze together with your hands. You can also use tennis balls or something similar. Set up a practice plan:

- *3 x 20 repetitions*
- *2 x 1 minute without a break*
- *3 x 30 seconds squeeze as fast as you can*

Strong and flexible wrists
For this exercise you first have to build a suitable training device. Take a wand or a stick (similar to a hockey stick). Attach a 40-inch piece of strong cord to one end. Attach a small weight to the other end of the cord.

Hold the stick with both hands like a hockey stick. Now wind the cord with the weight around the stick by twirling and swinging it. You can do this exercise outside, inside, standing up or sitting down.

MONITORING ONE'S PERFORMANCE

It is fun to follow one's performance development and (hopefully) track the progress. Trainers have charts and lists with standards and record performances for girls and boys in different age groups for many tests and competitions. Or compare your results with those of your training buddies.

The results can be shown with a diagram. Surely you are familiar with this type of diagram from your math or physics class. If you have any problems, ask someone to help you. The best way to do this would be together with your training group.

Get some graph paper and draw diagrams. The graduation of axis x for time can be in weeks or months. The graduation for axis y depends on the discipline you want to record, for instance seconds for sprinting or minutes for running, as well as the number of repetitions.

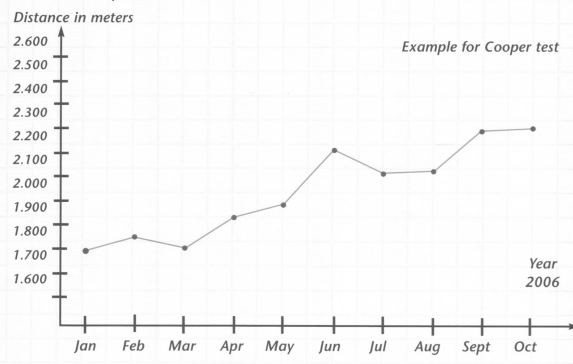

56

Flexibility

This is often also referred to as **agility**. It is apparent in how far an athlete can flex and extend his joints, and the range of motion his tendons, muscles and ligaments can tolerate. Of course, this also has something to do with age and build, with your strength, coordinative abilities and the elasticity of your tendons. But it is primarily a matter of training.

A field hockey player must maintain and continue to work on his flexibility. It is absolutely critical for the low body position, the deep lunges and the sometimes spectacular actions to reach a ball.

Good agility and flexibility guard against painful injuries from over-stretching!

There are many exercises for stretching everything from head to toe. You will find some of them in this book. But before you begin with the exercises, don't forget to warm up. Cold muscles and tendons are susceptible to injury when stretched a lot.

FLEXIBILITY EXERCISES

Don't forget: Don't start the exercises until after you have warmed up!

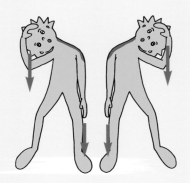

Stretching the neck muscles
Stand with your legs in a straddle position and lean your head to one side. The one hand gently pushes against the head and the other hand pulls toward the floor. Then switch sides.

Stretching shoulders, back and arm muscles

• Place your free hand around your shoulder or your elbow and pull the arm as far back as you comfortably can.
• For the second exercise, the arm is behind the head and you push the elbow toward the floor.

Stretching chest, back and shoulder muscles
The torso is bent forward and the hands are placed on a banister, the back of a chair or a table. Now push your torso down toward the floor.

Stretching the back
Sit back on your heels. Point your toes. Now reach really far forward with your arms and relax.

Stretching the lower back

Sitting on the floor, bend the right knee and keep the other leg straight. The left arm pushes lightly against the outside of the bent leg. Torso and head turn slowly to the right. Switch sides!

Stretching the hamstring

Lie on your back, hold on to your leg with both hands and pull the knee to the chest. The other leg is straight. Now flex the toes on both feet.

Stretching the gluteus muscles

Sit up straight, put the soles of your feet together and pull your feet close to your body. Now slowly drop your knees to the outside. Push against the inside of your knees with your elbows.

Stretching the quadriceps

Stand up straight and bend one knee back. Now pull lightly on the ankle. The hip must remain straight. To keep your balance you can hold on to a wall with one hand.

Hold each stretch for at least 10 seconds. Remember: It should pull but not hurt. After practicing for a while, you will notice that it keeps getting easier. You can find many more exercises in various books and sports magazines.

WARMING UP – STRETCHING – LIMBERING UP

Regardless of whether you are running or doing supplementary fitness training, want to do exercises at home or are at a tournament – this rule always applies! It is important that you prepare your body for the impending strain. At the end of the school day or after a restorative rest, your muscles are still relatively cold and stiff, and your breathing and pulse are still in "normal mode." Gradually, everything is prepared for training and the game. Once things get started, your engine will already be warmed up and well prepared.

Warming up

As the phrase suggests, you are getting warm! A variety of exercises help to get your muscles activated, improve their circulation and get them ready to perform. An indication for this is limberness, flexibility, a slight reddening of the skin and perspiration. It is a way to prevent injuries such as sprains.

Any movement that gets you going is good for warming up:
Jogging, easy jumps, calisthenics, ball games – even some light running, dribbling, passing the ball back and forth with a teammate, and shooting at goal.

All training sessions begin with the warm-up. That also goes for doing exercises at home or when you are late for practice. You can jog a few laps, do some jumps or jump rope by yourself.

Stretching muscles

Flexibility is increased primarily by stretching the muscles. You cannot just strengthen one muscle alone, but always have to keep in mind the antagonist, the "opposing player."

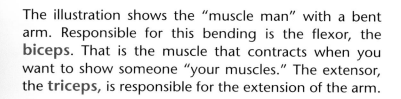

The illustration shows the "muscle man" with a bent arm. Responsible for this bending is the flexor, the **biceps**. That is the muscle that contracts when you want to show someone "your muscles." The extensor, the **triceps**, is responsible for the extension of the arm.

Feel your muscles! If you push down on a tabletop with your hand, the triceps gets hard because it wants to extend the arm in the elbow. The biceps is soft because it is relaxed and yields. But if you push against the table from below, the biceps is hard and the triceps is soft.

Limbering up

Although you have warmed up and stretched sufficiently, the muscles are often stiff and tense after a strenuous practice. After you have finished stretching, it is important to loosen up. Most of the time, you do these exercises automatically. You shake out your arms, legs and hands and move your joints gently in all directions. Easy jogging or jumping can also help you loosen up.

This preparation time not only gets your muscles warmed up and your entire body moving, but your head also adjusts to the impending strain. You shake off all your worries and problems.

HAVE YOU HAD A LAUGH TODAY?

TOM SAYS TO TINA: "YOU ARE WEARING ONE BLUE AND ONE YELLOW SHOE!" TINA REPLIES:
"YES, I THINK IT'S STRANGE, TOO.
AND I HAVE ANOTHER PAIR JUST LIKE THAT AT HOME!"

TWO PLAYERS COLLIDE WHILE RUNNING AND FALL DOWN IN A TANGLE.
ONE SHOUTS OUT: "HELP, HELP! I CAN'T FEEL MY LEG!"
THE OTHER ONE SAYS: "OF COURSE NOT, YOU KEEP PINCHING MY LEG!"

MR. SMITH WALKS INTO A SPORTS STORE.
"HELLO! I'D LIKE A HOCKEY STICK FOR MY DAUGHTER."
THE SALES CLERK ANSWERS: "SORRY, BUT WE DON'T DO MAKE TRADES!"

TOM ASKS MAX: "DID YOU BREAK UP WITH JULIE BECAUSE SHE WEARS GLASSES NOW?"
MAX ANSWERS: "NO, SHE BROKE UP WITH ME THE FIRST TIME SHE PUT HER GLASSES ON!"

"WHAT WOULD YOU DO IF YOU COULD PLAY HOCKEY AS WELL AS I DO?"
"TAKE LESSONS!"

TWO PLAYERS FROM ONE TEAM TALK AFTER THE GAME.
ONE SAYS: "THAT WAS A GREAT GAME TODAY.
TOO BAD YOU DIDN'T SEE IT!"

.7 TACTICS

WHAT ARE TACTICS

The word tactic is originally a military term. It referred to the manner of fighting, the deployment of troops and the specific use of weapons.

In common usage, tactics refers to planned actions to achieve a certain objective. In doing so, you think about how you – alone or as a group – can proceed step by step and which necessary means must be applied.

Look at our example from everyday life. Do you see yourself?

Max got a bad grade at school and has to find a way to tell his mother.

First he cleans his room, then he takes out the garbage, and then he helps his mother set the table. He casually tells her about the botched test, and by sheer coincidence he happens to have it with him, along with a pen for her signature.

Fortunately she did not get too upset!

Does that sound familiar? It's perfectly normal. To succeed one has to find an opportune situation, wait for the right moment, or do some preparation before the request for more allowance or a new CD. In other words, you proceed tactically.

TACTICS IN FIELD HOCKEY

Do you remember your first game or your first attempts at playing? Do you remember how all of you had to chase the ball – everyone wanted to get it and no one stayed in position? There was total chaos, everyone wanted the ball, and no one stayed in the rear for defense. A real game never actually came together.

However you are no longer such a beginner, but rather you train regularly at the club. Now you want to play well and in an orderly fashion with your teammates. So say good-bye to wild chaos, and hello to a tactical game.

Two types of tactics

Attack tactics These are all of the plays a team makes when it has possession of the ball.

Defense tactics These are all of the plays a team makes when the opponent has possession of the ball.

HOW NOT TO DO IT:

WHAT CAN WE DO ABOUT THOSE TWO TOUGH DEFENDERS ON THE OPPOSING TEAM SO WE CAN FINALLY GET INTO THE SHOT CIRCLE?

SIMPLE! GIVE ME A QUICK SIGNAL WHEN YOU'RE READY TO RUN TOWARD THEM. THEN I'LL KNOCK THE STICKS OUT OF THEIR HANDS.

THE TACTICAL USE OF TECHNIQUES

In a game, you have many different attack and defense techniques at your disposal.

What you choose depends on:

The situation

The situation, the distance to the goal and the positions of the players are quickly determined. After that, you decide (or together with a teammate) which technique to execute.

Where are the teammates? Am I being pressured by the opposing defense? Should it be a pass or a shot at goal?

Your personal performance capacity

What you have practiced often and well in training, you would of course like to use in a game. But don't take any chances and only use the techniques you feel sure about.

Can I make a shot at goal from this distance? I'm good at driving. I'm too slow for dribbling.

The strengths and weaknesses of your opponent

Find the opponent's weaknesses and use them to your advantage.

This player can't stop hard balls; I'll use that to my advantage! This opponent is difficult to dribble around; I better pass to my teammate! We need to pick up the pace because the opposing team is tired! We'll play the left; that's their weak side!

ONE TECHNIQUE AND MANY OPTIONS

Once you have chosen a technique (i.e., flicking the shot at goal while the goalie is still in a straddle postion on the ground), you can choose how to execute the technique. You can vary the technique in the way you hold the stick, swing and in the speed of the motion.

Fast – slow – hard – temperate, high – low with deception.

Attack tactics

- An attack plan is only successful if it matches the player's technical and fitness-related abilities.
- Most importantly, only use the technique you are best at.
- Be aware of your teammates' abilities!
- Pay attention to the opposing defense's strengths and weaknesses!
- Try to deceive the opponent!

Defense tactics

- Good defense is a prerequisite to a successful attack.
- Defense can only be successful if defender and goalie work well together.

Actions without the ball

- How can I get in position / get myself open?
- Observe and cover the opponents and interfere with their passes.
- Where can I help the defense?

TACTICS – THE PLAN FOR VICTORY

Tactics are a team's course of action or plan and the individual players' tasks contained therein that will hopefully beat the opponent in a game. We differentiate between *team tactics*, *group tactics* and the *tactics of the individual player* in specific positions.

Individual tactics

As a player you are in your position, following the game and watching the ball. At your disposal is an entire repertoire of techniques that you have learned at practice and now want to use successfully.

Group tactics

As soon as you connect with one or more teammates in a game, it is called group tactics. In an actual game situation, the team play is quickly clarified and tasks are divided up. This is done mostly via eye contact, calling out or "sign language."

Team tactics

For the tactics of an entire team, it is important that all players know what they have to do in their positions during certain situations. You are aware of your team's technical and fitness-related qualifications, and you know what every player is capable of and how well you all play as a team. Together with the trainer, you adjust your team tactics accordingly. In addition, there is the assessment of the opponent's strengths, weaknesses and preferred play and deliberation on how you best react to them.

SUPERIOR NUMBER

Probably the most successful way to win a game is a clever game of superior number. With fast and variable passes, the opponent will see you as unpredictable. You can cleverly dribble around him and the way to the goal is wide open!

But the various superior number ratios (2:0, 3:1, 3:2, etc.) don't usually arise coincidentally, but rather the players try to create this situation by getting themselves open.

You need to:

• Be smart about getting oneself open
• Employ group tactics
• Make quick decisions during the actual play

Superior number 2:1

A situation with two attackers against one opposing defender is most certainly the most common of superior number ratios in field hockey. If these two attackers play tactically smart, they can successfully outplay the defender.

The player with the ball has a teammate running along with him. The defender has to anticipate two situations:

He may be dribbled around or the ball may be passed to the teammate.

Variations

- The player controlling the ball is on the left. He dribbles the ball or makes a backhand pass to the right.
- The player controlling the ball is on the right. He dribbles the ball or makes a forehand pass to the left.
- The player controlling the ball is on the left. He dribbles the ball or makes a forehand pass to the left.

Player in possession of the ball

- He watches the defender and forces him into an initial action.
- If the opponent allows it, he simply passes or dribbles around him.
- If the defender prevents him from dribbling around him, the ball is passed to the accompanying player.

Accompanying player

- He runs, slightly ahead or behind, alongside the player controlling the ball at the same speed.
- He is very alert and always ready to receive the ball.
- The stick is carried close to the ground.
- The ball is not stopped when received, but carried along with the momentum.

This is how you can practice
- *Two players pass the ball back and forth diagonally or laterally.*
- *A cone serves as the "opponent" who must be outplayed.*
- *A passive opponent stands there without attacking.*
- *A passive opponent suggests his reach but does not attack.*
- *An active opponent tries to fend off the ball as in a real game.*

Accompanying at the right speed, timely passing, and receiving and passing the ball at a run are the requirements for a successful game. This should be practiced in all possible variations!

PERCEPTION FUNCTION

A field hockey player is fast. You want to be ready in any situation and react effectively. To do so, it is important to watch the action and the reactions of the opponents, your teammates' positions and their readiness to receive a pass, as well as seeing the path to the ball.

Are you able to grasp so many small and important details in a very short period of time? Take a close look at the photo on page 73 for 10 seconds (count to 10)! Try to memorize as much as possible. Now try to answer the following questions from memory!

1 How many players do you see in the photo?

_____

2 Is the ball more on the right side of the picture or the left?

_____

3 Which team does the player with the ball belong to (color of uniform)?

_____

4 With which side of the stick (forehand or backhand) is he playing the ball?

_____

5 Where do you see one of his teammates?

_____

6 How many spectators are shown?

_____

.......8 MENTAL ABILITIES

Why is it that humans can feel joy and sadness, that they can fall in love or hate someone? Why are people able to think, remember and dream?

People have always been curious about what goes on inside our bodies. No one had an explanation, so they called the whole thing the **soul**. The famous physician Rudolf Virchow (1821-1902) once asked his students to find the souls in the human body. But what they found inside the bodies they dissected were the brain, the heart, the lungs, the liver, and all of the other organs. They did not find a soul.

Of course they could not have found it, because our ability to perceive and imagine, think and decide, and feel and want are the result of our brain's activity. The science that deals with this is called **psychology**, and the old term "soul" was replaced by the word "**psyche.**"

Thus mental, or **psychological abilities**, refers to the field hockey player's ability to handle joy, anger, rage, excitement, competitiveness, fear and the many other emotions, and to advantageously and successfully apply them in training and during games. In psychology, research is also being done on how the thinking process works and how our muscles receive commands. We imagine our brain as a computer that controls everything. While you are playing field hockey your "computer" is working at high capacity, which is why it needs to be well prepared.

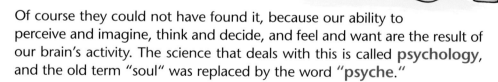

OUR "COMPUTER"

We don't want to turn this into a medical lecture. Besides, the brain as a topic is much too complicated and extensive to cover in a short chapter. But some people really think that sports are just about muscles. They don't know that the muscles' impulses originate in the brain, and that every complex athletic movement and action is controlled by nerve connections in the brain. In order for you to understand the importance of your brain in playing field hockey, we definitely could not leave a chapter like this one out of this training book.

PERCEPTION – CIRCUIT – BRAIN – MUSCLE

The illustrations show a simplified version of how this process works. You receive lots of information via receptors located in your sensory organs. You can see, hear, taste and feel things.

Nerve tracts then carry this information to the brain. On the way to the brain, the information first ends up at a circuit. In our illustration, this is a piece of bone marrow located in the spinal column. The brain then sends an "order" to the respective muscle, telling it what to do.

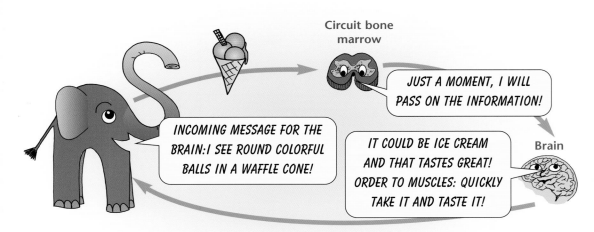

Conscious reaction

Most impulses and information we receive via our senses are relayed from the circuits to the appropriate section of the brain. After the incoming impulses are checked, they are compared with experiences and mentally processed. The orders travel along the nerve tracts from the cerebral cortex via the spinal cord (that was the circuit) to the muscles for the execution of the conscious actions.

Perception:	You see a hard and shallow ball coming in.
Your experience:	When it comes in like that I can't stop it with a high stick!
Mental preparation:	I get ready to receive the ball by "laying a plank."

Pretty difficult! But don't worry, most of this will come when you train properly and have gained some experience.

Reflexes

Are you familiar with the following situations? You accidentally touch a hot stove top and quickly pull your hand away, or you are blinded by bright light and squeeze your eyes shut, or you slip on a slick surface and flail your arms to keep from falling. In these situations, your muscles react automatically, without your having to think about what to do. This reaction is called reflex. Because you don't have to first think about what to do, the information does not have to be forwarded to the brain. The impulse goes from the circuit straight to the muscle.

In field hockey, these phenomena occur when, for instance, the ball suddenly comes in differently than expected or an unexpected chance for a shot at goal arises. Then you have to react quickly and don't really have time to think. Thus a player can be in control of any situation.

When you play a lot, especially with different players from the team and against different opponents, you gather experiences and develop your reflexes.

At the same time, you should know as much as possible about your sport. A field hockey player can decide much quicker what a particular impulse means and how to best respond to it if he is well prepared and doesn't have to spend a lot of time thinking about it.

YOUR MENTAL STATE AFFECTS YOUR PERFORMANCE

You prepare for a tournament by training a lot. You continuously work on your fitness level and refine your technique. You get tips, correct mistakes and practice until you've got it. Now you are exceptionally well prepared and should just have to do everything the way you do it at practice. But what's going on? You are shaking with anxiety, you are afraid you'll fail, miss the ball or hit it out of bounds. You can barely concentrate on the game. Are you now hopelessly at the mercy of your feelings and trembling legs, or can the psyche be trained as well?

It is very important to know exactly what is going on inside of you. When you know the causes, you can adapt yourself more easily and prepare for such situations.

Tension and nervousness

Nervousness before a competition is normal and important. No athlete can be successful if he is totally relaxed and laid back about everything. This inner tension helps you to perform at your best. However, too much nervousness is bad. You cannot concentrate as well, are stiff and – most importantly – you make mistakes.

Fear

There are different reasons why a player may be afraid. Sometimes it is fear of reacting badly and failing. Hard balls or aggressive play by certain opponents can at first also be intimidating. Maybe you even made some stupid mistakes recently or you're not sure you are good enough for your team and may be criticized? A little respect is very useful. It makes you more serious and vigilant. Otherwise, a fearful player is unsure of himself and lacks the necessary bite. Talk to your friends or your trainer. Relaxation exercises are often helpful.

Anger

You can be angry at many things – your trainer, your teammates, your parents, your girlfriend, the opponent, school, etc. Maybe the technique didn't work out as well at training or in a game as you had anticipated. Are you sometimes angry at your teammates, opponents who play dirty, or the referee? You must learn to deal with aggressive feelings. Don't make your teammates or trainer the focus of your anger. If you feel angry, use that feeling to tackle the task at hand with more focus and spirit. Be forceful but not unfair! Stay calm and use it as an incentive.

Talking to yourself a little can often help with your concentration, give you courage and spur you on!

Perseverance

A player will always be in situations where he is nervous, afraid or angry, where he pushes himself to the limit or is just plain unenthusiastic. He should be able to tough it out at practice, get better and, when necessary, grit his teeth and bear it. Always look for new challenges and be ready to try something new. You will meet your limits time and again, and must learn to push past them in a sensible way.

Such challenges include the following examples:

Fear of hard balls.
("I can't stop that ball properly. It'll be too hard!")

Limited physical capacity in training.
("I can't go on, it is too strenuous!")

Fear of new things.
("The way I used to do it always worked so well! Why do I have to try something new now? Surely it won't work out!")

Conflict with trainers or training buddies.
("It's always my fault! No one notices my difficulties and helps me!")

Get over your fears and you will be proud of yourself later. Perseverance in sports toughens you up and also helps you cope with problems at school and in other areas of your life.

Attentiveness and the ability to concentrate

Whether there is commotion at the edge of the field, people are shouting or the opposing team is happy about scoring a goal – don't get distracted! The athlete must completely concentrate on the game. Thoughts about private issues, fear of possible mistakes or losing are distracting. Problems at school or what to wear to the next party should also be disregarded during practice or a tournament.

The more difficult a task, the more you should concentrate on it. When your thoughts wander you won't be able to react to the ball fast enough, you'll miss a pass and you'll get slower.

Tips for improving attentiveness

To be attentive, you have to want to!

When you don't really feel like concentrating on the game, every little thing will distract you. Before you begin to concentrate, tell yourself why you are doing it and what it is good for.

Don't let anything or anyone distract you!

Concentrate on the game, the ball and the other players. Even just looking to see what the spectators are doing can lead to a mistake.

Take a concentration break!

Your ability to concentrate is not endless. Every person has to rest and renew his strength!

Even the best athlete loses sometimes!

If you're too slow, don't have enough strength, hit the ball out of bounds, or the ball came in too hard and slid over your stick, you'll ask yourself why it happened. Maybe you were out of form, the team isn't well established yet, or the opponents were older than you. Don't get angry, but keep training! If you're good, you'll do better next time. Be happy about personal progress and successes.

 If you think you should have done better, think about the reasons and causes and, together with your trainer, determine methods for your continued training.

SELF-CONFIDENCE

Some say, "Self-confidence is half the battle!" Of course it isn't quite that simple, but there is some truth to that saying. Someone who approaches a task with self-confidence, joy and pep, who believes in himself and his form certainly has a better chance at success than someone who is afraid and full of doubt.

HE, HE! YOU GUYS ARE NO MATCH FOR ME! YOU DON'T STAND A CHANCE AGAINST MY HITS! WHAT ARE YOU CLOWNS EVEN DOING HERE?

But you shouldn't get reckless and make a mistake because you are overly confident!

OH BOY! IT'S NOT GOING TO WORK OUT AGAIN! I'M JUST PLAIN BAD AND I ALWAYS MISS THE BALL. WHEN I SEE THE OTHERS. I JUST WANT TO GO HOME!

Which of the following qualities and attitudes can you, as a field hockey player, benefit from, and which are more of a hindrance? Cross out anything you don't want to have too much of.

Self-confidence – joy in playing the game – self-doubt – blind rage – willingness to take risks – impatience – being laid-back – fear of making mistakes – ambition – desire to win – faith in one's performance – pessimism – bad mood – feeling in great form – attentiveness – concentration

RELAXATION EXERCISES

To relax, find a quiet spot in the locker room, at the edge of the field or in the gym, where no one will disturb you. Sit or lie down and close your eyes. The most important part is proper breathing.

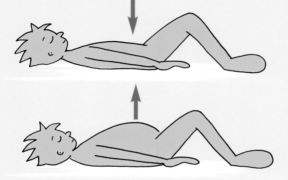

Exhale calmly and slowly. The abdominal wall retracts.

Inhale deeply into your stomach. The stomach extends.

The following exercises will stretch muscles and tendons. You will feel a slight pulling. That's good, but it shouldn't hurt. Hold the position as long as you comfortably can. No bouncing! Don't forget good belly breathing when doing the following exercises! You can find more exercises in yoga books.

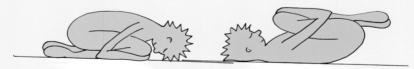

Make yourself really small, like a little package.

Get on your back and extend your legs back over your head.

From a kneeling position, sit back on your heels and then lean really far forward.

SELF-IMPOSED PRESSURE ON THE FIELD

What do you think of this story about Jennie? Does it sound familiar?

Jennie has been looking forward to the tournament. She has told everyone how well things are going at practice and that the trainer has put her in the lineup for the team. She was well prepared. She packed her bag the night before and checked off everything on her checklist. Now it's early to bed to get rested up for the big day! But then everything goes wrong at the tournament. The passes are off, when she receives passes, the ball bounces too far away from the stick, and her opponents seem to outplay her effortlessly. Everyone is surprised and wonders what is going on with Jennie today.

What happened to Jennie is something that can happen even to very successful athletes during important games.

The pressure was too much; she was too nervous, could not concentrate and was not able to give her usual performance. While it isn't the end of a career, it is very annoying!

You should know why such a situation occurs and what you can do about it.

PRESSURE

PRESSURE AFFECTS HOW YOU PLAY

On the one hand, external expectations influence pressure. They come from your parents, your trainer, the club, school and your friends. They all expect you to perform well.

BRAVO, YOU ARE THE BEST! WE'RE PROUD OF YOU! TODAY YOUR DEFENSE WILL BE GREAT! SHOW THEM WHAT YOU CAN DO!! WE'RE COUNTING ON YOU!!

I WANT TO SCORE GOALS TODAY! I'M GOING TO SHOW THEM! I'M GOING TO REACH EVERY BALL! EVERYONE WILL BE PROUD AND CHEER! ALL THAT TRAINING IS WORTH IT!

And then add to that your own expectations. You want to reach the goals you set for yourself.

Sometimes the pressure of these expectations is too much. You become afraid of not being able to meet the expectations of others or your own. And that's stressful!

How to deal with pressure

- **Get well prepared for the tournament during the week at practice.** Train diligently and concentrate. Prepare yourself properly for the demands that await you. Then nothing that happens will be a surprise.

- **Get everything ready the night before**, double check everything, go to bed early, eat a good breakfast and leave your house on time.

- **Leave behind all problems that have nothing to do with the game.** Imagine that no other problems can touch you once you're on the field. Only concentrate on the ball and the action.

- **You chose the pressure yourself.** You set the goals and determine what you want to achieve. Of course you could also set goals that are easier to reach and avoid the pressure by "deferring" to teammates, not wanting to win anyway, or by not even joining the team. Set high but realistic goals for yourself. A little pressure is necessary. It's fun, spurs you on and gets you moving.

- **Pressure builds character!** You will only get strong if you can handle pressure situations. Each time you will be able to handle more pressure. Someone who already avoids pressure in the preparation phase will become a "weakling" and will always fall short of his potential. Conquering your fears will strengthen your character.

Watch successful athletes as they relax and concentrate before a game and during breaks. How do they react to mistakes, a change in the game situation, successes or defeats?

Try to emulate them and find out what works best for you. Practice these rituals and carry them out again and again. Character traits you develop through playing field hockey will also be useful in other areas of life!

TEST

How would you react in the following situations?

1. Situation: You don't feel like going to practice.

A Of course you stay at home because you shouldn't force yourself. 1

B You go to practice without much enthusiasm because you don't want to disappoint your parents. 2

C You go to practice like you always do because missing practice will make you get worse again. Maybe you will feel better once you get to the gym. 3

2. Situation: The trainer repeatedly criticizes you for not having your stick on the ground when receiving a ball.

A It is irritating that I'm still doing it wrong. But I'm happy just to reach the ball. 2

B He shouldn't be so petty all the time. It's not a beauty contest. One more word and you're leaving! 1

C It's good that the trainer is always watching. That way certain mistakes won't be able to creep in at all. 3

3. Situation: Your opponent appears to outplay you effortlessly during a one-on-one in the first half and easily enters your team's shot circle.

A Your breathing is calm, and you concentrate on the defense. 3

B You think that won't happen again in the second half. You take a look to see if all your relatives are there and wave to them. 2

C You are afraid you'll "mess up" the game. It has already been preprogrammed that you don't have a chance against your opponent. 1

4. Situation: Last week the trainer told you that Tom will start on the team instead of you.

A You think, too bad, maybe I just wasn't good enough. 2

B You are upset because you are at least as good as Tom. Hopefully he won't do well and you can say: "I would have been better!" 1

C You help Tom and support him in everything he needs. You work hard during practice so you will start again next time. 3

5. Situation: The ball keeps bouncing up every time you try to accept a shallow pass from your teammates.

A It makes perfect sense. I was blinded by the sun and couldn't see the ball. 1

B That's pretty annoying. But now I'll quickly focus on the next ball. 3

C The game is almost over and my concentration is fading. 2

6. Situation: You see another player strike your teammate's stick.

A You accept the call and keep on playing. 3

B You approach the opposing player and ask him to be fair and report it. 2

C You ask yourself if the referee "has blinders on" and verbally harass him. 1

Add up your points! You will find your score in the solutions section.

1 Do you have enough imagination?

There once was a little bug in love, and it crawled along a ribbon to get to his true love. Will he make it, or will he end up on the wrong side of the ribbon?

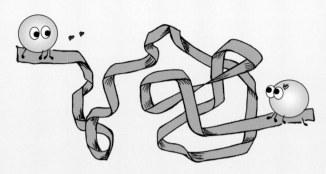

2 What's the code?

Draw the remaining symbols so that each symbol appears only once in each row, each column, and each diagonal!

3   **Connections**

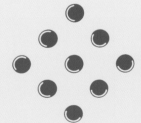

Connect these nine dots in one stroke with straight, continuous lines!

4 Matches

By moving only three matches you get three squares of equal size. Try it!

86

.....9 RECEIVING THE BALL, CONTROLLING THE BALL, SCORING A GOAL

To make a field hockey game possible, the players must be able hold and move the stick correctly. For this, they assume the typical body position. Now the players need the necessary techniques so they can properly receive and control the ball, pass it to a teammate, defend it from the opponent, and of course score goals.

You have already learned and continued to improve the most basic techniques during your initial years of playing field hockey. We have described these in detail in the beginner book "Learning Field Hockey." In coming years, you will continue to improve and refine these techniques and learn additional options.

In this chapter, we would like to briefly review the beginning techniques and then build on them. We will describe additional techniques, offer information on particulars, possible mistakes and exercises.

The top field hockey players in the world have a giant repertoire of playing techniques that they learn and continuously refine in the course of their athletic careers.

THE MOST IMPORTANT ACTIONS IN FIELD HOCKEY

This chart shows the most important techniques a hockey player can use in particular situations.

CONTROLLING THE BALL

RECEIVING THE BALL

- Forehand and backhand with vertical stick

- Forehand and backhand with low stick

- Receiving high balls

- Receiving bouncing balls

- Pulling the ball

- Lateral forehand control

- Forehand shinnying

- Frontal forehand control

- Backhand control

- Forehand/backhand control

- Curve left/right

- Stopping from lateral forehand control

DRIBBLING AROUND

- "Laying the ball" past a player

- Sliding the ball through a player's legs (Tunneling)

- Over the sideboards (Only indoor)

On the following pages we will briefly describe the techniques you likely already learned in the beginning and are already familiar with from the first book.

You will find additional select techniques on the subsequent pages.

DEFENSE

PASSING THE BALL

GOAL SHOT

- Defensive jab
- Defensive block
- Forehand/backhand steal

- Push pass
- Push / hit
- Forehand hit
- Forehand drive
- Scoop pass
- Flick
- Short grip hit
- Low drive

- Push pass
- Push/hit
- Forehand hit
- Forehand drive
- Scoop
- Flick
- Short grip hit

THE BODY POSITION

Over the long time that people have been playing hockey, a particular body position has developed. It is how the players can run fastest, control the ball most ably and pass it most reliably.

Ready position

The player stands erect, feet about shoulder-width apart, and the stick is held with both hands horizontally in front of the body. He follows the game in this position when he doesn't have possession of the ball. Thus he is ready at any time to run to the ball or receive a pass.

Playing position

The player has a low body position; the left hand is at the top of the stick and the right hand is several hand-widths below the left. The eyes should be taken off the ball often to keep an eye on the situation or to seek out a teammate to pass to, as well as an open space or an opportunity for a shot at goal. It is in this position that the player moves with the ball, receives it or passes it on.

As soon as the ball comes near you, set the stick down on the ground! This prevents the ball from moving past you before you even have time to react.

THE STICK POSITION

In hockey, the stick is the most important instrument and is an extension of the arm. That is why you have to handle it securely and skillfully. It must be held so it won't fall from your hand and follow the ball after a hard hit. But the hockey stick must also be maneuverable enough so you can quickly turn and move it. That is important because the ball can only be played with the flat side of the stick.

Rotating the stick

To quickly switch from forehand to backhand and from backhand to forehand, the left hand holds the stick and determines the direction of rotation. The right hand does not participate in the rotating motion. It is like a grommet that guides the screw and keeps it from slipping.

In forehand position

The ball is positioned to the left of the stick on the flat side.

In backhand position

The ball is positioned on the right side of the stick.

But since the ball can only be played with the flat side of the stick, the stick must be rotated for the backhand. The tip of the blade now points down.

RECEIVING THE BALL

Receiving the ball with a low stick

If the ball comes in quietly, without bouncing and shallow, it is best to stop it with a low stick. This allows you to use the entire length of the stick to receive the ball.

Forehand stop
"Laying a plank"

Backhand

Receiving the ball with a vertical stick

If you want to receive a high and bouncy ball, it is better to broaden the receiving surface vertically.

Receiving laterally

Receiving frontally

Low stick

When receiving the ball with a low stick, you increase the width of the receiving surface.

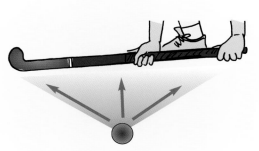

Make sure the gap to the ground isn't too big, so the ball won't roll through it.

Always tilt the stick towards the ball, or the ball may bounce up against your body.

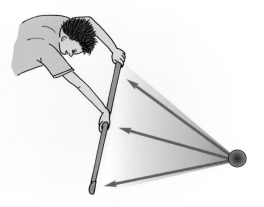

High stick

When receiving the ball with a high stick, you increase the height of the receiving surface.

Make sure that the gap to the ground isn't too big, so the ball won't roll through it.

Catch the flying ball "with your eyes" and stand steadily and securely before receiving the ball.

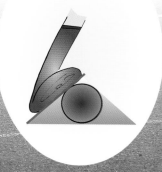

Roofing

You will receive the ball more reliably if you hold the flat or vertical stick tilted slightly forward (45°). With this roof position, you can stop the ball and it won't bounce over your stick.

Little backhand

This receiving technique is somewhat specialized and not that easy to learn. But someone who has mastered this technique can utilize the many opportunities in a game, particularly when attacking on the right side. You can win many one-on-one situations with this good receiving technique, and thus quickly shape the game, especially when it comes to steeply played passes. The ball can be received while standing still or moving.

Whenever you are to receive a steep pass, you should face the direction of the incoming pass. Look over your right shoulder, position your little backhand and await the pass. Here, too, the ball is received approximately level with the left foot, and when positioning the stick you have to remember to make a roof.

Once you have safely received the ball with the little backhand, immediately rotate the stick to the forehand position and look straight ahead in running direction.

- *The player awaits the pass in a crouched position.*
- *The back is turned to the ball.*
- *In a stride position, the left leg is forward in the direction of play.*

- *The stick is slanted forward.*
- *The player looks over the right shoulder at the passing player.*

Stick position

To be able to successfully receive the ball, the player must be aware of some important things.

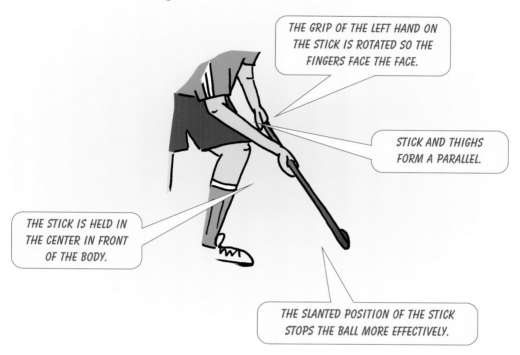

THE GRIP OF THE LEFT HAND ON THE STICK IS ROTATED SO THE FINGERS FACE THE FACE.

STICK AND THIGHS FORM A PARALLEL.

THE STICK IS HELD IN THE CENTER IN FRONT OF THE BODY.

THE SLANTED POSITION OF THE STICK STOPS THE BALL MORE EFFECTIVELY.

- The ball is received approximately level with the left foot.
- The roofing of the stick or a slight tap against the incoming ball makes stopping the ball easier.
- You can also push the stick to the ground and stop the ball with the shaft of the stick.

PASSING THE BALL

What makes a pass a good pass? It is on target, with the appropriate force and good timing. That sounds logical, but in a game it is quite a challenge. To do so you have to closely observe the action and the intentions of your teammates, as well as the opposing defense. Based on that you choose the appropriate technique and at the right moment pass precisely on target.

Hard passes are often easier to receive than gentle ones.

Push pass

A push pass allows you to pass the ball quite accurately over shorter distances.

After the pass, don't just let the stick "swing out." (You might injure another player.) Once the ball leaves the stick, you have to "fasten down!" This makes the pass harder.

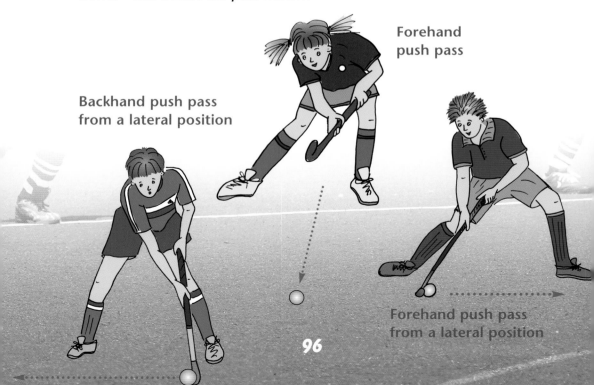

Forehand
push pass

Backhand push pass
from a lateral position

Forehand push pass
from a lateral position

The drive

Very important is that the driving technique can only be used in field hockey.

It allows you to play the ball very hard and cover a great distance. The drive is suitable for a long pass to a teammate, for the opening hit, a free hit or a shot at goal.

- *The ball is centered in front of the body, so that the stick can be held at about a 45° angle.*
- *The feet are shoulder-width apart.*
- *The player switches from rotation grip to hitting grip.*
- *The hands are close together on the stick.*

- *The tip of the blade points up.*
- *The eyes are on the ball.*

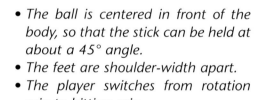

- *After the backswing a high degree of acceleration must be achieved.*
- *The drive does not solely result from strength, but primarily from the swing.*

97

The low drive

This hitting technique developed with the introduction of artificial turf. This stroke is therefore also often referred to as "turf stroke."

Phases of execution: **Backswing**
Accelerate
Strike
Finish swing

- *During the backswing, the player goes into a deep, wide lunge with the left leg.*
- *The blade is open to the top.*
- *The left shoulder points in the direction of the drive.*

- *The ball's acceleration begins with the setting down of the left foot.*
- *The body's center of gravity moves down.*
- *At the same time, the stick makes a looping motion.*

The grip

The **left hand** is the leading hand. Coming from the left, you grip the flat end of the stick with it. It thus leads the backswing motion and determines the angle of the stick.

Coming from the right, the **right hand** grips the stick directly below the left hand. This hand is the power hand, which carries out the motion.

Your hands must not interfere with each other, but must work together.

> THE LEFT WRIST IS RIGID AND EXTENDED.

> HAND PRESSURE IS STRONG AND FIRM, BUT NEVER CLENCHING THE STICK.

After hitting the ball, don't just let your stick swing out, but actively slow it down. This allows you to increase the ball's accuracy and hardness.

- *The stick moves level above the grass.*
- *The ball is struck with maximum acceleration (like a whip).*

- *After the strike, the motion is slowed down.*
- *Body weight shifts from the right to the left foot.*

MISTAKES YOU SHOULD AVOID
WHEN DOING THE LOW DRIVE

The low drive is an important field hockey technique. If the drive comes at the right moment, is on target and has the right momentum, the opponent has trouble fending it off.

Look closely at the motion sequence and the tips on the preceding pages, and keep monitoring the individual phases while practicing.

Which mistakes are these players making with the low drive?
You will find the solutions to these pictures in the solutions chapter.

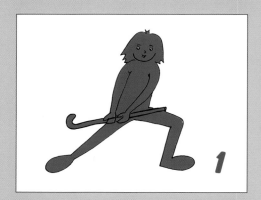

List any additional mistakes that can occur and those you definitely want to avoid, on the blank lines.

_____

_____

_____

The short grip hit

In international tournaments, the game keeps getting faster and faster. Actions like the short grip hit continue to become more important.

Due to the shorter grip on the stick, the backswing phase has become shorter as compared to that with the "normal" grip. But this also means that, due to the shorter acceleration phase, more effort is required.

It takes much less time to complete the entire action. This means that the opposing defender also has much less time to interfere with your hitting the ball and fending it off.

You can really surprise the opponent with this hitting technique.

- *The feet are shoulder-width apart.*
- *The hands are close together on the stick, slightly lower than the low drive. The left hand slides down more on the stick, and the right hand slides up.*
- *Hips are flexed, knees are bent and the left shoulder points in hitting direction.*

- *The elbow initiates the backswing motion.*
- *The torso twists and the weight is on the rear foot.*

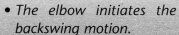

Top players adapt their playing technique to the opponent's style of play. A faster game requires a faster technique!

Phases of execution: **Starting position**
Backswing
Strike
Finish swing

- *During the strike, the body's center of gravity goes down and the left foot is planted firmly on the ground.*
- *During the strike, the body weight is shifted to the right leg.*
- *At the moment when stick and ball connect, the player stands firmly and his center of gravity is in the center.*

- *The stick swings after the ball.*
- *During the final phase of the swing, the body weight is on the front foot.*

103

The hit

This technique is particularly well suited for opening hits. The ball can be passed to the teammate very accurately and on target without the backswing motion. But this type of pass can also be very hard, like a drive. It is also a good way to feint passes.

Phases of execution: **Backswing**
Accelerate
Strike
Finish swing

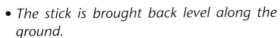

- *The stick is brought back level along the ground.*
- *The stick's blade is open to the top.*
- *At the point of return, the wrists are tilted back.*

- *During the acceleration phase, the extreme knee bend causes the torso to come down very low.*
- *The player takes a big sliding step with the left leg at ball level.*

Measuring

If the player has sufficient time, he can "measure" the distance before the backswing. To do so, he suggests the swing and "tests" the strike.

The particulars

A player executing a hit can be compared to a hammer thrower. He swings the stick like a hammer thrower swings his hammer in a throwing competition. (But don't forget: In field hockey, the stick stays in the hand!)

- *Due to the extreme knee bend, the torso comes down very low during the acceleration phase.*
- *The player takes a big sliding step with his left leg at ball level.*

- *After the ball is struck, the rotation slows down.*
- *The stick is dragged a little farther across the ground.*

The flick

Flicking is a technique in which the ball is also raised during the forward movement. This technique is used, for instance, for the execution of 7-m balls on a small field or in field hockey.

It is a way to play the ball over a goalie lying on the ground, or as a pass to a teammate through the free space over a tight defense.

In indoor field hockey the ball can only be played low – no flicks allowed! Here you can use the flick only for shots at goal.

- *From the starting position, the player goes into a wide straddle stance.*
- *The left foot is forward.*
- *The ball is on a level with the left foot and so far away from the body, that the stick angle is about 45°.*

- *The pushing motion is initiated by a shift of the body weight from the right to the left leg.*
- *The stick approaches the ball parallel to the feet.*

Phases of execution: **Starting position**
Strike
Lift
Push

Stick position

How high the ball travels depends on the position of the stick. The more angled the stick is relative to the ball, the higher it will go. Important is that you find the right pressure point.

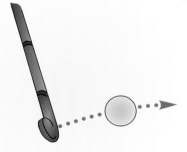

- *The leading hand brings the end of the stick forward to the left knee.*
- *The stick approaches the ball parallel to the feet.*

- *The flat side of the stick is directly behind the ball.*
- *The right hand pushes the blade with the ball forward and up.*
- *The lower the weight is shifted, the steeper the ball's trajectory.*

107

THIS IS HOW YOU CAN PRACTICE PASSING

A pass is successful when the ball safely reaches a teammate. To do this, the player in possession must have a very good feel for passing at the right moment, the exact direction of the pass and the required effort in order to be accurate. But of course that can be practiced!

Against a wall

The player finds a wall (Be careful! Don't play against windows, freshly painted surfaces or noisy garage doors).

- *You play against the wall and receive the returning ball.*
- *Alternate playing the ball harder, gentler, a little to the right, a little to the left.*
- *Change the distance – increase or decrease the distance.*

Passing

Two players stand facing each other and play the ball back and forth.

- *They pass the ball back and forth so it is easy to reach.*
- *Play the ball harder, gentler, a little to the right or to the left.*
- *Change the distance – longer or shorter distance.*
- *Play through a marking that gradually gets narrower.*

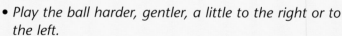

Use different types of balls: Field hockey ball, tennis ball, softball, etc. It is a way to work on your stick-ball feel.

Into a goal

The player marks a goal with a tire or a piece of string forming a circle.

- You play the ball low and so accurately that it stops in the goal.
- You flick the ball. It should land in the goal.
- Change the distance – longer or shorter distance.

Proper flicking

There are some exercises to get the feel for the motion and thus the correct lifting of the ball. To start, you lay the ball on one edge of a table or some other raised surface.

- Using your hand like a spoon, you bring the ball forward with your hand and play it up into the air. You need to have the right speed and your hand at the right angle for this.

- You play the ball forward from the edge with the stick and raise it up at the same time. You need to have the right speed and your hand at the right angle for this.

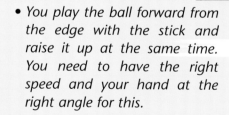

- Kneel on the floor with your stick and play the ball from a kneeling position.

DRIBBLING AROUND SOMEONE

Simply dribbling around a player or pretending to do so is a very important technique in field hockey. It is a way to achieve promising superior number ratios, thus creating scoring opportunities.

The sequence

Preparation

- The ball is brought in front of the body and controlled there.
- A position is reached from which it is possible to play in all directions.
- To have good control, the ball has to stay close to the stick.

Dribbling around a player

- Execute the action at lightning speed.
- The ball is played past the opponent.

Continued play

- The ball is protected.
- Move away from the opponent as fast as possible.

Dribbling around the opponent works particularly well when he is in ready position with his feet in parallel position. This makes it more difficult for him to turn around quickly and run in the other direction.

Dribbling around a player forehand and backhand

You choose the forehand or backhand, depending on whether you want to dribble around the opponent on the left or the right.

Dribbling around forehand

- You approach your opponent controlling the ball frontally.
- In front of the opponent, you play the ball forehand to the left.
- You follow the ball and quickly move away from the opponent.

Try to "entice" the opponent to use his backhand!

Dribbling around backhand

- The attacker dribbles around the opponent on his backhand side.
- You approach your opponent, controlling the ball frontally.
- In front of the opponent, you play the ball backhand to the right out of the opponent's reach.
- You follow the ball and quickly move away from the opponent.

Once you have successfully dribbled around the opponent, "step on the gas" and quickly run away!

"Pulling" the ball past the opponent

In this variation of dribbling around a player the ball is controlled frontally, and when meeting the opposing defender, it is played past his backhand side. You yourself pass him on the forehand side to resume playing the ball behind the opponent.

Since the opponent will most likely focus more on your body movements, you will catch him "on the wrong leg."

- *You slowly approach your opponent.*

- *He will attempt to take the ball from you with the "plank" he laid.*

- *Now quickly push the ball past the opponent's backhand side.*

- *But you suddenly run quickly past the opponent's forehand side.*

Always make sure that the opponent doesn't read your intentions. The more he is caught off guard, the more successful your action will be!

Tunneling

The opponent is trying to steal the ball to launch his own attack. He sees you coming, and wonders whether you will try to pass him on his forehand side or backhand side. You take advantage of his uncertainty, and if there is room, play the ball through the opponent's legs.

- *You slowly approach your opponent.*

- *He will try to determine whether you will want to pass him on the left or the right.*

- *Now he chooses an appropriate defense technique and assumes a wider stance.*

- *You take advantage of this and push the ball forehand through his legs.*

- *You quickly pass the opponent, take the ball and immediately resume play.*

Take advantage of your opponent's surprise and remove yourself and the ball from the opponent as quickly as possible!

113

Over the sideboards

This option for dribbling around a player can of course only be used in indoor hockey, where there are sideboards.

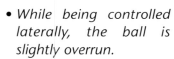

- *While being controlled laterally, the ball is slightly overrun.*
- *You must entice the opponent to use his forehand.*
- *The push pass passes the opponent on the right, and hits the sideboard.*

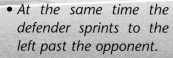

- *At the same time the defender sprints to the left past the opponent.*
- *He takes the rebounding ball.*

Feinting (dekeing)

Of course no opponent will allow you to run to the goal with your stick on the ball. He will want to interfere and take the ball away to launch his own attack. You have several options to either run away from the defender or to dribble around him. But he will attempt to read your intentions and quickly react to them.

But you can also just feint a certain action, your opponent will move in the wrong direction, and you're home free.

Some such feints are:

Feinting with your eyes (You look in one direction and play in another.)
Body feints (You move your torso in the wrong direction.)
Feinted movements (Backhand / forehand, forehand / backhand)

• *Backhand play is suggested, but then the ball is played forehand.*

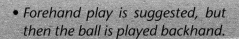

• *Forehand play is suggested, but then the ball is played backhand.*

THIS IS HOW YOU CAN PRACTICE DRIBBLING AROUND ANOTHER PLAYER

Someone who wants to successfully dribble around another player needs to be able to execute important movements confidently, quickly and skillfully.

Bringing the ball in front of the body from a lateral position

The action of dribbling around a player always takes place from a frontal position relative to the opponent. That's why it is very important that you bring the ball quickly and securely from the lateral to the frontal position, i.e., in front of the body.

- *From a slow run*
- *From a fast run*
- *Quick switch at an obstacle or on demand*

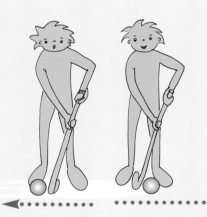

Playing the ball to the right or the left from a standing position

If you play the ball too far to the right you will miss it, and if you play it too short the opponent will get it.

- *Play the ball to the left or the right at a marked target.*

From a run, play the ball to the left or right side.

During plays you often want to dribble around the opponent at a full run.

- *Play the ball at a run to the left or the right from the marking, or on demand.*
- *Play the ball to the right or the left at a marked target.*

Practicing against a passive opponent

For this exercise set up poles, cones or other obstacles that you can dribble around forehand or backhand.

Practicing against a partially active opponent

Partially active means that an "actual" opponent is standing there, but he does not interfere and disrupt your dribbling. So your partially active opponent does not have to be a field hockey player. Parents, younger siblings or other "fearless volunteers" would be fine.

Practicing against a partially active opponent who "suggests" his reach

Your "opponent" doesn't interfere but he suggests the extent of his reach. To do so he may, for instance, lay a plank or go into a lunge. But he cannot drag his rear foot.

Practicing against an active opponent

An active opponent doesn't just stand there but instead tries to prevent you from successfully dribbling around him. Like a real opponent, he will attempt to take the ball away from you so he can become the attacker.

117

MISTAKES YOU SHOULD AVOID WHEN DRIBBLING AROUND ANOTHER PLAYER

Loss of the ball, poor passes or rule violations are most often the result of a flawed technique. Error analysis means that when problems occur during a game or in practice, the player thinks about why they happened and what the causes were.

The trainer and teammates will also help recognize mistakes. Observe one another, point out each other's mistakes, and practice together.

Photos or video footage taken by parents or the trainer during practice sessions or at games can often be helpful. It is a way for you to really see your technique.

In these pictures we show commonly occurring mistakes. Do you recognize them?

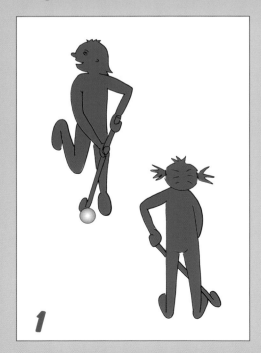

List any additional mistakes that can occur in field hockey below! What do you have to pay particular attention to?

_____

_____

_____

_____

_____

_____

SHOOTING AT GOAL

For a field player the greatest thing is to successfully shoot the ball into the goal and thus contribute to the victory of his team. Every field hockey player knows that it isn't that easy.

The sequence:

- Penetrate the opposing shot circle.
- Create a favorable opportunity for a shot at goal, most often through team play with teammates.
- Recognize an opportunity for a shot on the opposing goal.
- Seize the same with determination.

A prerequisite for this is mastery of the various passing techniques (that are also used to shoot the ball into the opposing goal) and to be able to use them confidently in the appropriate situation.

Here, too, applies the old saying: No sweet without sweat!

Once you have penetrated the opposing shot circle, you have already achieved a great advantage over your opponent. For your opponent, it's a "red alert" when you have played yourself into his shot circle. The opponent knows that if he makes a mistake at that moment, you and your team will score a goal, a penalty corner or a 7-m penalty shot. If your team is unable to successfully conclude the attack, it is irritating, but it doesn't change the score.

If you want to use the goal shot in a competition, you must practice it intensively, just like all the other field hockey techniques. That is why shots at goal are often a part of team training.

Techniques for the goal shot

- Push pass
- Push hit
- Forehand hit
- Forehand drive
- Scoop
- Flick
- Short grip hit

But you can also practice goal shots, outside of team practice, alone or with field hockey friends.

To practice goal shots, you will need:

- A hockey field with a hockey goal to be able to practice under realistic conditions with accurate distances and lines.

- A safety fence or net behind the goal, or it will be dangerous for others. If you always have to chase after the balls and look for them, you waste too much time.

- You need a field hockey ball, but it would be even better if you have several balls to practice with. Ask your trainer when you can use the hockey field for practice and where you can get balls to practice with.

THIS IS HOW YOU CAN PRACTICE THE SHOT AT GOAL

It is often better to be able to practice and train with friends. If your team's goalie wants to practice with you, you can simultaneously work on his goalie defense techniques and your goal shot exercises.

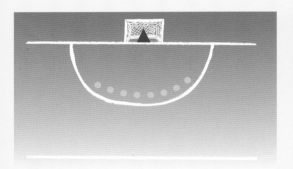

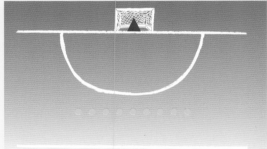

Goal shot from the shot circle

Several balls are placed at the edge of the shot circle and hit or flicked into the goal from there.

Goal shot with running start from the quarter line

Several balls are lined up at the quarter line. You start with the ball at the quarter line and take it into the shot circle, and then hit, push or flick it, perfectly placed and hard, from the edge of the shot circle into the goal.

- *The balls can be played high or low.*
- *Position some gym bags or other obstacles between the goal line and the 7-m point.*

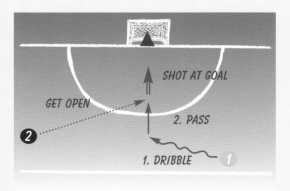

Direct goal shot

Player 1 dribbles the ball and then plays it into the path of Player 2.

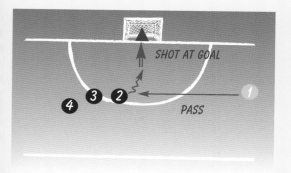

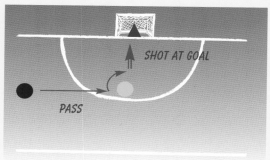

Shot at goal after receiving the ball

Player 1 passes the ball. After briefly "pre-blocking" and making contact with the ball no more than twice, Player 2 (3, 4) hits the ball into the goal.

Goal shot after a pass from the left

The ball is passed from the left. After the ball is received a brief turn follows, and then comes the goal shot with a short grip hit.

Try executing the hit while falling down sometimes!

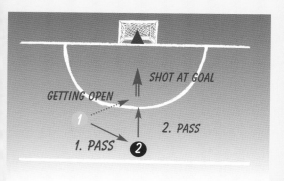

Shot at goal after a pass from the back

Player 1 plays the ball to the back to Player 2 and runs forward, getting himself open. The pass from the back is received with a little backhand, and the goal shot is carried out with a forehand drive.

In individual training it is also very important that no one gets hurt! Talk to your trainer about this as well. He will certainly be able to give you some good advice.

Don't forget to warm up!

DEFENSE

To play field hockey successfully, your team needs to first of all have possession of the ball. That is why the team and each individual player's defensive skills are very important.

The better the defense, the greater the pressure on the opponent! The sooner you can successfully mount a defense, the faster you are in the opposing shot circle! That is why defense techniques are not only important for defenders, but also for the midfielders and forwards.

The defender does not have many options for bringing the ball into his possession. The rules only permit the hockey stick to be used for playing the ball. So he has to wait for the right opportunity to take the ball with the forehand or backhand or intercept it. Most of the time he can manage to get the ball when the attacker plays the ball too far ahead, doesn't have it under control or makes a bad pass.

Keep in mind:

- The objective of defensive play is to stop the opposing attack, fairly separate the opponent from the ball without a violation, and then immediately launch a counter-attack.

- The defensive player must be patient, but then act quickly and decisively at the right moment. When one wants the ball very badly, one often takes the first step and is thus more likely to be outplayed!

- Staying at optimal reaching distance prevents the dribbling around the left foot, i.e., with the backhand.

- The lower the defender's center of gravity, the greater is his reaching distance.

Defensive block forehand

- *The defensive player stands facing the attacker in possession of the ball as much as possible and assumes a very low stance.*
- *He attempts to quickly and accurately determine the ball's path.*

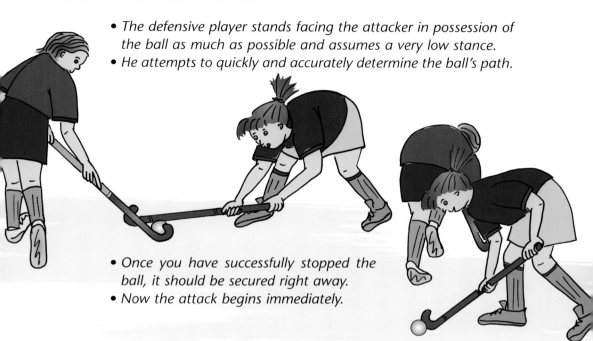

- *Once you have successfully stopped the ball, it should be secured right away.*
- *Now the attack begins immediately.*

The stick does not hit the ball but blocks the ball's path!

Defensive block backhand

- *While backing up, the ball is stopped with a low backhand.*
- *At the same time the stick's blade points down (backhand plank).*

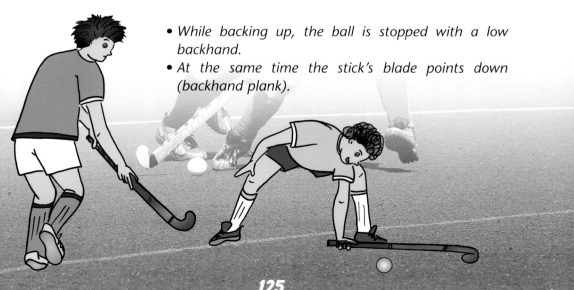

Accompanying

The defender tries to "take the ball away" from the attacker. To do so he runs alongside the attacker and waits for an opportune moment to fight for the ball. Such an opportunity arises for instance, when the opponent plays the ball too far ahead, or you can guess where he wants to pass.

- *The defensive player pressures his opponent with his forehand without lunging at the ball.*
- *You move along in the opponent's running direction at his speed, and at an opportune moment you successfully employ the defense techniques.*

Stealing the ball forehand

- *The defender is on the right of the attacker in possession of the ball.*
- *He accompanies him and waits for an opportune moment.*
- *The blade is carried along the ground.*
- *At the right moment, the blade is moved in front of the ball.*
- *The ball is first pushed to the left of the running direction.*

Make sure you don't have too much speed when you "dock" to the opponent.

Employ the following defense techniques calmly, deliberately and not hectically, but with determination!

Avoid getting into too much of a frontal position with the opponent. Otherwise he can easily outplay you (e.g., over your left foot) or "tunnel."

Stealing the ball backhand

- *The defender is on the right of the attacker in possession of the ball.*

- *He accompanies him and waits for an opportune moment.*

- *He rotates the stick to the backhand position, holds it only with the left hand and brings the blade close to the ball.*

- *The ball is stolen from the attacker with a brief pushing motion to the right.*

MISTAKES YOU SHOULD AVOID IN DEFENSE

Not all means are allowed in defense and for stealing the ball. It is important that you know the rules and can use the permitted techniques well.

Take a close look at the two drawings. What mistakes are the defenders making?

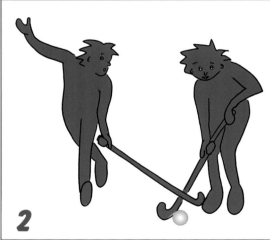

What can be the reason when you make the following mistakes in defense?

1 *When stealing the ball, it stays within the opponent's reach.*
2 *You don't make contact with the ball during the defensive movement.*
3 *The opponent intercepts the ball.*
4 *A stick violation is called.*
5 *The attacker plays around you.*

Defensive jabs

You use the defensive jab when you are certain that you can "jab" the ball away from the opponent. It is a brief, quick movement without a prematurely recognizable preliminary motion.

Basic position

- *Left foot and left shoulder are turned towards the opponent in possession of the ball.*
- *The weight is on the left leg with a low center of gravity.*
- *The feet are approximately shoulder-width apart.*
- *You stand at reaching distance (= stick length + arm length + lunge) to the ball.*
- *The left hand holds the stick (like a frying pan) with the stick surface facing up (open blade). The right hand is approximately one hand-width lower.*

Execution

- *Body, arms and stick face in direction of the ball.*
- *The lunge initiates the movement and precipitates all of the subsequent movements.*
- *The torso and left arm catapult the stick in the ball's direction. At the same time, the right hand releases the stick.*
- *The ball is jabbed from below (the stick's point of impact is directly in front of the ball), so that it bounces out of the opponent's control.*

Feint defensive jabs

But you can also just feint the defensive jab to pressure the opponent. To do so, only the arm and stick move in the direction of the ball, while the body moves away. After the feint jab, the defensive player immediately returns to the basic position and the right hand returns to the stick.

THE GOALIE

The goalie has a very special place on the team. This is not only apparent by the special gear, but also because he often has to face the opponent alone.

A goalie must react quickly and be skilled and flexible. In addition he needs lots of courage and self-confidence. Most of the time he doesn't have much time to think during a dangerous situation but has to react with determination and without hestitation.

And when a ball goes in anyway? That can happen! It is important not to spend a lot of time thinking about it but to immediately get ready for the next situation!

The goalie has several defense options. He can clear the ball:

With the body.

With his hand.

With the shin guards.

With the stick.

With the kickers.

Clearing with the hand

The goalie can clear high balls with his free hand or with the stick.

To **clear with the hand on the left side**, the goalie lifts his hand to the side. The ball is cleared with the palm of the glove so it bounces down or to the side.

To **clear with the hand on the right side**, the goalie brings his hand up vertically and then over his head to the right. The palm of the glove points in the direction of the shot and intercepts the ball.

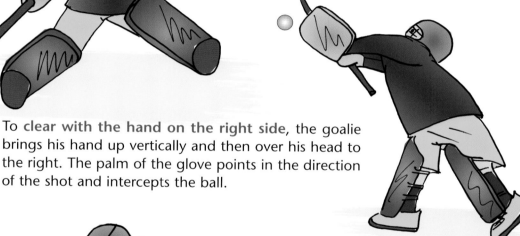

The goalie can also clear the ball **with the glove on the stick hand**. The glove's palm points in the direction of the shot and the ball should bounce sideways to the right.

Clearing with the foot

If the incoming ball is low, it can be cleared with the foot or kicked away. In doing so, the goalie always shifts his weight to the supporting leg.

Stopping

The goalie has the option to stop the ball with the bottom of his foot or the inside or outside of his feet, as well as trapping it between both feet. If the ball goes in the corner of the goal, the goalie can usually reach it only with a wide straddle.

Every goalie should be able to clear well with both legs. Playing soccer is a good exercise, whereby you can specifically use your "weaker" foot.

Kicking

Kicking means playing the ball with your feet. For this the goalie can use the tip of his toes, or the inside or outside of the foot. The kick is executed from a standing position after stopping the ball, from a standing position with a backswing or at a run. When kicking with the inside of the foot the goalie gathers more momentum than when kicking with the outside of the foot.

- *The playing leg swings back and kicks the ball next to the supporting leg.*
- *As you kick, you pull your knee forward and up.*
- *During the backswing, the foot is rotated out and the toes come up.*
- *The ball connects with the inside (instep) of the foot.*

A kick with lots of momentum is very forceful; a kick with less momentum is more accurate.

Clearing with the stick

High, medium-high, or low balls on the goalie's right side can be cleared with the stick.

- *The stick is held on the right side.*
- *The flat side of the stick faces the ball.*
- *The stick does not move while clearing the ball.*
- *The stick is tilted slightly forward and down, so the ball bounces down or to the side.*

Clearing with shin guards

Low and knee-high balls can be cleared with the shin guards. From the ready position, the goalie rotates his leg out slightly and then extends it towards the ball.

Combination clearing

The goalie also has the option of combining clearing techniques. This allows him to increase the size of the clearing area.

Hand-stick-clearing

This clearing technique is suited for balls that come in at hip or shoulder-level. For balls coming in on the stick side, the goalie uses the catching hand on top of the stick. For balls on the hand side, the goalie holds the stick's backhand above the catching hand.

Foot-hand-clearing

A ball at approximately hip level on the left side can be cleared with a foot-stick combination. To do so, the shin guard moves to the ball and the inside of the hand is held directly above.

Foot-stick clearing

Balls that are played on the goalie's right side at approximately hip-level can be cleared with a foot-stick combination. The shin guard moves to the ball and the stick is held directly above the shin guard.

134

Goalie positioning

Successfully utilizing the defense options requires clever positioning by the goalie.

The shot angle

When the goalie stays on the goal line, the shooter has lots of room to score a goal. If he stands farther out in front of the goal, he can decrease the shot angle, and the attacker has fewer opportunities to shoot the ball past him.

You can see in the illustrations how the goalie can decrease the shot angle.

Ready position

The goalie watches the game and the actions of the attackers and his defenders. He assumes the ready position in anticipation of a shot on goal. From this position, he will be able to react quickly.

- *The feet are about shoulder-width apart and the weight is on the ball of the foot.*
- *Knees, hips and elbows are slightly bent.*
- *The stick is in the right hand and the flat side of the stick faces forward.*
- *The palm of the left glove faces forward.*

135

O	P	R	M	P	O	T	A	T	O	E	S	E	B
Z	U	C	C	H	I	N	I	W	L	T	M	R	I
S	V	N	M	Y	L	M	S	C	I	W	O	T	X
Q	D	M	G	Y	R	O	C	I	H	C	W	F	Z
U	M	R	E	B	M	U	C	U	C	Y	U	O	I
A	N	A	P	R	T	Y	M	O	W	O	K	T	H
S	X	N	W	S	G	V	L	R	N	M	P	A	C
H	I	A	V	K	G	I	Y	U	C	X	W	F	A
P	I	N	A	P	P	L	E	M	S	E	Z	M	N
S	N	A	R	W	H	L	E	T	T	U	C	E	I
K	Z	B	P	E	P	P	E	R	S	K	T	W	P
P	E	A	R	W	C	A	R	R	O	T	L	S	S
G	R	A	P	E	S	W	F	L	E	M	O	N	I
K	I	W	I	Y	R	R	E	B	W	A	R	T	S

Fruits and vegetables are healthy!

Find 17 fruits and vegetables – horizontally, vertically or diagonally, forwards and backwards!

Oh, Dear! Always such excitement before the game!

Which is the quickest way to the restroom?

Can you trace the route?

TOM ASKS HIS FRIEND: "HOW HIGH IS THIS BARRIER?" HIS FRIEND CLIMBS UP, MEASURES AND CALLS DOWN: "FOURTEEN FEET!" TOM REPLIES: "YOU'RE SO DENSE! YOU COULD HAVE JUST WAITED FOR IT TO COME DOWN!" ANSWERS THE FRIEND: "BUT I WANTED TO MEASURE HOW HIGH IT IS AND NOT HOW WIDE!"

. . . .10 HEALTHY ALL AROUND

Anyone who thinks that hard, sweaty training several times a week is enough for athletic success will soon learn the better. Next to the demanding training, periods of recuperation are very important; also plenty of sleep, good nutrition, physical hygiene, organization, and much more.

You should be familiar with your internal clock and learn to pay attention to it. It tells you when you are particularly fit or when you urgently need rest and should relax. A good field hockey player, for instance, also senses when he needs some high-energy nutrition to maintain his performance capacity and concentration.

In this chapter we have compiled some interesting information on this topic. Take this as an incentive to learn more about your body and your internal clock, as well as good nutrition.

Have fun!

OUR PERFORMANCE CAPACITY

In the course of a day, our performance capacity experiences highs and lows, as you can see on the curve below. This is similar for all people, and we have adjusted our lives accordingly. Most school instruction is done in the morning, then some people even take a nap during lunch, in the afternoon we accelerate again, and at night our body gets its well-earned sleep. Anyone who follows this rhythm lives a healthy and productive life. You can feel it if you don't get enough rest and sufficient sleep, and it would be a shame not to utilize those physical "highs."

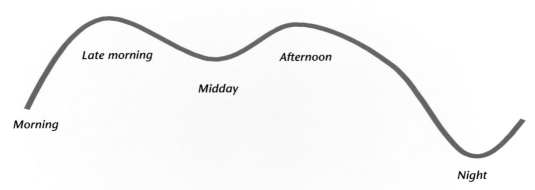

EAT AND DRINK YOURSELF FIT

Athletes who eat or drink too much or the wrong things before training are not efficient. They feel stuffed and appear tired and listless. Many body functions slow down because the stomach is working overtime. But we must eat and especially drink to replenish the body's used up energy and to balance the loss of fluids caused by sweating. It is also necessary to do so periodically during long training sessions and competitions.

Look at this overview to see what is (and is not) suitable for your main meals, snacks, and the in-between energy boost. Choose your foods and drinks, as well as the time of consumption so you are sufficiently satiated during training or at a tournament and are not still digesting.

How long foods stay in the stomach until they are digested:

Approx. one hour: | Water, tea, broth.
Approx. 2-3 hours: | Cocoa, banana, apple, roll, rice, cooked fish, soft boiled egg, whole grain bread, cake, buttered bread, Muesli, vegetables.
Approx. 4-5 hours: | Sausage, meat, fried potatoes, French fries, beans or peas.
Approx. 6-7 hours: | Layer-cake, mushrooms, fish in oil, fatty roast.

Don't forget to drink!

To balance the loss of fluids from sweating, you have to drink enough fluids during training and competition. Otherwise your performance capacity drops, your blood thickens and absorbs less oxygen, and you will get muscle cramps.

● **Suitable beverages before and during exertion**

Water, juice and water mix in proportions of 1:3, lightly sweetened beverages.

Don't choose beverages that are really cold because the body has to expend lots of energy to warm it up.

● **Suitable beverages after exertion**

Juice and water mix with a higher juice ratio, milk smoothies, and beverages with higher sugar content.

139

ENERGY SOURCES

You are only capable of extreme physical exertion if you intake sufficient energy (sugar/starch) in the form of nourishment. If you have absorbed a sufficient amount you achieve optimal performance capacity. Not enough causes a drop in efficiency, lack of concentration and fatigue. But with too much energy absorption there is a danger of extreme nervousness and quick exhaustion.

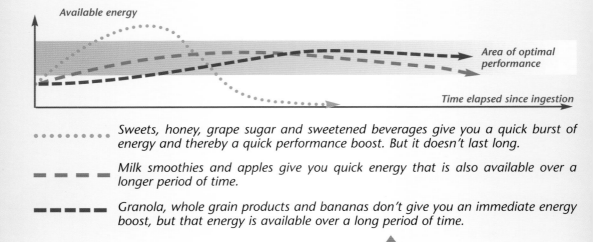

Sweets, honey, grape sugar and sweetened beverages give you a quick burst of energy and thereby a quick performance boost. But it doesn't last long.

Milk smoothies and apples give you quick energy that is also available over a longer period of time.

Granola, whole grain products and bananas don't give you an immediate energy boost, but that energy is available over a long period of time.

The food pyramid shows which foods you should eat in large quantities (very bottom) and which you should preferably eat very rarely (very top). Examples are given for each food group.

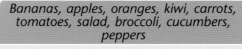

Layer cake, chocolate candy, chocolate, candy

Milk, cheese, yogurt, sausage, meat, eggs, beans, peas, nuts

Bananas, apples, oranges, kiwi, carrots, tomatoes, salad, broccoli, cucumbers, peppers

Bread, potatoes, rice, noodles, Muesli, cornflakes

Water, juice and water mix, tea, whey

140

ACCIDENT PREVENTION AND FIRST AID

Playing sports is good for your health! You strengthen your cardio-vascular system, your muscles, bones and joints. Training and playing with the team is fun and promotes a sense of community. But to keep it fun there are some things, in addition to good nutrition, that you need to pay attention to.

So nothing bad happens

Warming up

By warming up, you get your heart and breathing going, increase your muscle temperature, and your tendons and ligaments are slowly stretched. You reach "operating temperature."

Strengthening and stretching

A well-trained and strong body, strong muscles and joints, as well as pre-stretched tendons and ligaments can handle heavy strains better. The risk of injury is thus lower.

Regeneration

After strenuous training and games, it is important to "cool down" slowly and gradually. This allows the body to slowly recuperate. The high "operating" temperature is gradually reduced. It is also a way to avoid or reduce muscle soreness.

Protective gear

Clothing
- Wear proper athletic shoes that lend good support to your feet when making quick movements and won't let you slide.
- Shin guards protect from unintentional strikes with the stick or from balls you can't stop.
- A mouth guard is particularly important.

Field
- The field or the indoor playing surface should be level, without places where you can trip or slippery spots.
- Side boards, cool-down area, safety nets behind the goal, lighting

When something bat does happen

Minor injuries can occasionally occur:
- Protect abrasions from dirt.
- Turning an ankle: **RICE**= **R**est – **I**ce – **C**ompression – **E**levate
- More severe injuries need time to heal. But that does not mean a total break from training. Rest the injured body parts and train something else in the meantime.

Only a healthy body can give an athletic performance. Get advice from your trainer and your doctor!

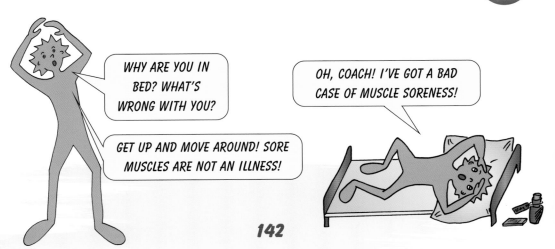

. . . . .11 SOLUTIONS

Pg. 26 **1.** You tell your trainer that the task is too difficult for you and you would rather practice from a standing position for a while longer.

2. You should tell your trainer that this is not challenging enough for you and you want to flick farther.

Pg. 70 You can look at the solutions in the photo and check your answers.

Pg. 79 **Our opinion**

Self confidence – joy in playing the game – ~~self-doubt~~ – ~~blind rage~~ – willingness to take risks – ~~impatience~~ – being laid-back – ~~fear of making mistakes~~ – ambition – desire to win – faith in one's performance – ~~pessimism~~ – ~~bad mood~~ – feeling in great form – attentiveness – concentration

Pg. 84/85

15-18 points
You can go far with your attitude about sports. You enjoy competition, are fair and have willpower. Keep it up!

10-14 points
You have a good attitude about sports but sometimes you move only in first gear. With more fun and the desire to win you could be more successful. Take the training and games seriously, be fair to the other athletes, and have more fun playing field hockey.

6-9 points
You mostly just think about yourself! You need to work on your attitude with respect to fairness and camaraderie.

Pg. 86   **1.** The little bug unfortunately did not reach his love.

2.   **3.**

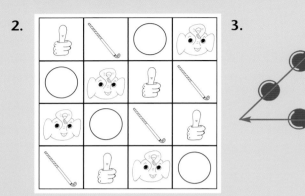

4.

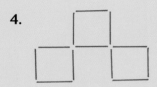

Pg. 100/101

Mistakes with the low drive

1   The stick is held in the middle instead of the end.
2   The eyes are not focused on the ball but in the direction of the backswing.
3   The blade points down
4   The body position is too upright.
5   The rear leg is extended.
6   The ball is hit high instead of low.

Pg. 118/119

Mistakes with dribbling around a player

1 The player in possession of the ball is distracted from the outside and does not concentrate on the action.
2 The defender is distracted from the outside and does not concentrate on the action.

3 The defender holds the stick too high.

4 While dribbling around the other player, the player in possession of the ball hits the ball too high.

Pg. 128

Mistakes with defense

1 The defender is not in ready position and is not focused on the action.

2 The defender doesn't play the ball with his stick but hits the opponent's stick instead. This counts as a foul.

1 The ball is not taken far enough away when stolen.

2 The blade of your stick is not on the ground.

3 The defense movement is too slow.

4 You try to hit the ball.

5 He can read your intention to attack too early.

Pg. 136

O	P	R	M	P	O	T	A	T	O	E	S	E	B
Z	U	C	C	H	I	N	I	W	L	T	M	R	I
S	V	N	M	Y	L	M	S	C	I	W	O	T	X
Q	D	M	G	Y	R	O	C	I	H	C	W	F	Z
U	M	R	E	B	M	U	C	U	C	Y	U	O	I
A	N	A	P	R	T	Y	M	O	W	O	K	T	H
S	X	N	W	S	G	V	L	R	N	M	P	A	C
H	I	A	V	K	G	I	Y	U	C	X	W	F	A
P	I	N	A	P	P	L	E	M	S	E	Z	M	N
S	N	A	R	W	H	L	E	T	T	U	C	E	I
K	Z	B	P	E	P	P	E	R	S	K	T	W	P
P	E	A	R	W	C	A	R	R	O	T	L	S	S
G	R	A	P	E	S	W	F	L	E	M	O	N	I
K	I	W	I	Y	R	R	E	B	W	A	R	T	S

145

. . . . .12 LET'S TALK

DEAR FIELD HOCKEY PARENTS!

It is easy to get excited about field hockey. Field hockey, whether it is played indoors or on the field, is a great sport.

Your child, too, has chosen this sport and has begun to practice. But now he wants to go on, train seriously in a club and get on a team.

Do you know why that is? Ask your child or have him show you the pages in the book that talk about motives. One thing you should understand: Someone who trains in field hockey wants to be successful, score goals and win with his team.

This training book focuses on young players in their initial years of training. It offers much information about their sport, about technique, tactics and how to train properly. The young people will learn to better realize their own potential and to more consciously work with their bodies. This does not only promote more effective training but also prevents possible under- or over-training.

The basic and intermediate training are the same for all young players, regardless of whether they will later remain recreational players or switch to successful clubs. For all of them, this book provides an orientation and support for successful training.

All parents, siblings, grandparents and friends receive important information. Use this book together with your children as a training companion, workbook and reference work. You will occasionally be asked to help design performance charts or keep notes. Together with your young field hockey player enjoy his personal achievements and successful games. Adolescents need our approval, praise and recognition. Be sympathetic on those occasions when things aren't going well. Not everyone has what it takes to be a world-class player.

More than anything field hockey is fun, promotes social interaction, and develops ambition and perseverance. As they train and play together, the children and adolescents learn to overcome their weaker inner self and learn to deal with success and failure. Character traits such as fairness, dependability, punctuality, organization, perseverance, the willingness to take risks, courage and team spirit are cultivated and are also useful in other areas of life.

DEAR FIELD HOCKEY TRAINER!

Good youth training focuses on the entire personal development of children and adolescents. It is considered a learning activity because it promotes the control and automatic control processes. It has a socializing effect because group training in particular practices social norms, rules and behavior patterns. Training for children and adolescents is stimulating and takes moods, perceptions and feelings into account.

It ensures positive experiences, processes needs and wishes, and is conducted in a warm, loving and open-minded atmosphere. The young field hockey players are your partners in this – providing they are actively involved in the training process and have enough freedom to act.

Therefore, don't view the young athletes as recipients of your instructions, but as partners in the mutual training process. Tell them why which exercise is necessary when, and which workload is particularly beneficial for which training segments. We would like to hereby hand the children a workbook that is a training companion. They can review things

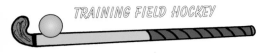

they have learned, as well as record goals, motives and their personal performance development. Of course, no book is a substitute for the years of experience a trainer has. Also, the opinions of trainers, sports scientists and authors sometimes differ.

Consider this training book a supplement and an aid in the involvement with the sport beyond the common training.

A good youth trainer always thinks about how he can use field hockey training not only to teach techniques or develop physical fitness, but also to actively involve children and adolescents in the practice and training process, so he can, aside from improving the quality of practice sessions, consciously foster the personal development of his players.

We wish you and your young field hockey players
continued fun and success.

PHOTO & ILLUSTRATION CREDITS

Cover design:	Jens Vogelsang, Aachen
Illustrations:	Katrin Barth
Cover photo:	Katrin Barth
Photos (inside):	Katrin Barth, Kerstin Dischereit, Wolfgang Quednau, Dieter Reinhardt (Lutz Nordmann), Dr. Wolfgang Sternberger (Tina Bachmann), Regina Weitz, Ulrike Sluga
Graphic art, pg. 12	Peter-T. Schulz "Olle Hansen" (Mülheim and der Ruhr, Germany)

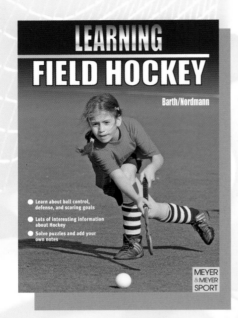